Who Feeds
REALLY
the World?

Who *Really* Feeds the World?

THE FAILURES OF AGRIBUSINESS
AND THE PROMISE OF AGROECOLOGY

Vandana Shiva

North Atlantic Books
Berkeley, California

Published by

North Atlantic Books   Cover design Jasmine Hromjak
Huichin, unceded Ohlone land   Book design by Suzanne Albertson
aka Berkeley, California

Cover art by Maria Sibylla Merian and Joseph Mulder, Moonflower (Ipomoea alba) with Passalus interruptus beetle and jewel beetle (Euchroma gigantea) and Pomelo or shaddock (Citrus maxima) with metamorphosis of moth (Urania leilus), 1719; Maria Sibylla Merian and Peter Sluyter, Duroia eriopila with zebra swallowtail (Eurytides protesilaus) and Xanthocleis psidii larva and pupa, 1719; Joris Hoefnagel and Georg Bocskay, Insects, Orange Lily, Caterpillar, Apple, and Horse Fly and Fly, Caterpillar, Pear, and Centipede, 1561-1562. Digital images courtesy of the Getty's Open Content Program.

Printed in the United States of America

First published as *Chi nutrirà il mondo?* in April 2015 by Giangiacomo Feltrinelli Editore, Milan, Italy.

Who Really Feeds the World? The Failures of Agribusiness and the Promise of Agroecology is sponsored and published by North Atlantic Books, an educational nonprofit based in the unceded Ohlone land Huichin (*aka* Berkeley, CA) that collaborates with partners to develop cross-cultural perspectives; nurture holistic views of art, science, the humanities, and healing; and seed personal and global transformation by publishing work on the relationship of body, spirit, and nature.

North Atlantic Books' publications are distributed to the US trade and internationally by Penguin Random House Publishers Services. For further information, visit our website at www.northatlanticbooks.com.

Library of Congress Cataloging-in-Publication Data
Shiva, Vandana, author.
  Who really feeds the world? : the failures of agribusiness and the promise of agroecology / Dr. Vandana Shiva.
  pages cm
  "An in-depth look at agroecology, an alternative to the world's current food crisis" —Provided by publisher.
  ISBN 978-1-62317-062-2 (pbk.)
  1. Food supply.   2. Agricultural ecology.   3. Agricultural industries.   I. Title.
II. Title: Failures of agribusiness and the promise of agroecology.
  HD9000.5.S455 2016
  338.1'9–dc23   2015034909

6 7 8 9 10 KPC 25 24 23 22

North Atlantic Books is committed to the protection of our environment. We print on recycled paper whenever possible and partner with printers who strive to use environmentally responsible practices.

To all the beings that give us food.
To Richa, for her editing.

Contents

Introduction ix

1. Agroecology Feeds the World,
Not a Violent Knowledge Paradigm 1

2. Living Soil Feeds the World,
Not Chemical Fertilizers 15

3. Bees and Butterflies Feed the World,
Not Poisons and Pesticides 27

4. Biodiversity Feeds the World,
Not Toxic Monocultures 41

5. Small-Scale Farmers Feed the World,
Not Large-Scale Industrial Farms 55

6. Seed Freedom Feeds the World,
Not Seed Dictatorship 67

7. Localization Feeds the World,
Not Globalization 85

8. Women Feed the World,
Not Corporations 111

9. The Way Forward 125

Endnotes 141

Index 157

About the Author 167

Introduction

We are facing a deep and growing crisis rooted in how we produce, process, and distribute our food. The planet's well-being, people's health, and societies' stability are severely threatened by an industrial globalized agriculture driven by greed and profits. An inefficient, wasteful, and nonsustainable model of food production is pushing the planet, its ecosystems, and its diverse species to the brink of destruction. Food, whose primary purpose is to provide nourishment and health, is today the single biggest health problem in the world: nearly one billion people suffer from hunger and malnutrition, two billion suffer from diseases like obesity and diabetes, and countless others suffer from diseases, including cancer, caused by the poisons in our food.[1]

Instead of remaining a source of nourishment, food has been transformed into a commodity: something to be speculated on and profiteered from. This leads to rising food prices and creates social instability everywhere. Since 2007 there have been fifty-one food riots in thirty-seven countries, including Tunisia, South Africa, Cameroon, and India.[2] The food system is badly broken on every measure that counts: sustainability, justice, and peace.

Today, an alternative has become an imperative for our survival, so let us begin by asking the question, "Who feeds the world?"

Food and agriculture have become sites for major paradigm wars. Under each paradigm, a certain type of knowledge, economics, culture, and, of course, farming is being promoted. Each paradigm claims to feed the world; in reality, only one does.

The dominant paradigm is industrial and mechanized, which has led to the collapse in our food and agricultural systems. This crisis is not an accident; it is built into the system's very design. At the heart of this paradigm is the Law of Exploitation, which sees the world as a machine and nature as dead matter. This paradigm sees humans as separate from nature, and every part of nature as separable from the rest: the seed from the soil, the soil from the plant, the plant from the food, and the food from our bodies. The industrial paradigm is also based on seeing humans and nature as mere inputs in a production system. The productivity of the Earth and its people is made invisible by a sophisticated intellectual infrastructure that puts the twin constructs of capital and corporations at the center of its economics.

The paradigm of industrial agriculture is rooted in war: it very literally uses the same chemicals that were once used to exterminate people to destroy nature. It is based on the perception that every insect and plant is an enemy to be exterminated with poisons, and is constantly seeking new and more powerful instruments of violence, including pesticides, herbicides, and genetically engineered pesticide-producing plants. While the technologies of violence grow more sophisticated, the knowledge of ecosystems and biodiversity shrinks. The deeper the ignorance of the planet's rich biodiversity and ecological processes, the greater the arrogance of corporate destroyers who claim to be creators. Life is thus redefined as an invention of those whose only desire and capacity is to poison and kill it.

Tools governed by the Law of Exploitation and the Law of Domination harm people's health and the environment. These tools are often poisons marketed as "agrochemicals," and we are told that farming is impossible without them. In reality the corporations that make these chemicals are shaping the paradigm of possibility. They define what constitutes scientific knowledge, what an efficient food production system looks like, and what the boundaries of research and trade should be. When applied to agriculture and the food system, a paradigm rooted in the violence of war and a militarized mindset brings the war to our fields, to our plates, and to our bodies.

But there is another new, emerging paradigm, one that maintains continuity with time-honored ways of working together with nature and is governed by the Law of Return. Under this law, all living beings give and take in mutuality. This ecological paradigm of agriculture is based on life and its interconnectedness. It is centered on the Earth and small-scale farmers, and especially women farmers. It recognizes the potential of fertile seeds and fertile soils to feed humanity and diverse species to whom we are all related as Earth Citizens. Under this paradigm, the role of the human community is to act as cocreators and coproducers with Mother Earth. Within this paradigm, knowledge is not owned; rather, knowledge grows through farming, where we are all participants in the web of life. In ecological agriculture, the cycles of nature are intensified and diversified so as to produce more and better food, while using fewer resources. In ecological farming, the waste of the plants becomes food for farm animals and soil organisms. Adhering to the Law of Return, there is no waste; everything is recycled.

Ecological food systems are local food systems, growing what they can, exporting real surpluses, and importing what cannot be grown locally. Sustainability and justice flow naturally from the Law of Return and from the localization of food production. The resources of the Earth that are vital to the maintenance of life, such as biodiversity and water, are managed as a "commons," or shared spaces for communities. The ecological paradigm cultivates compassion for all beings, including humans, ensuring that no one is deprived of his or her share of food.

Today, the industrial paradigm is in deep conflict with the ecological paradigm, and the Law of Exploitation is pitted against the Law of Return. These are paradigm wars of economics, culture, and knowledge, and they frame the very basis of the food crisis we are facing today.

———————

"Who feeds the world?" The answer depends on which paradigm we use as our lens, because the meaning of "food" and "world" vastly differs between the two. First, let's examine this from the perspective of the dominant paradigm: industrial, mechanized agriculture. Under this paradigm, "food" is a mere commodity to be produced and traded for profits, and the "world" is a global marketplace where seeds and chemicals are sold as farming inputs and commodities are sold as food. If the planet is seen through this lens, it is chemical fertilizers and pesticides, corporate seeds and GMOs, agribusiness, and biotechnology corporations that feed the world.

Yet the reality is that only 30 percent of the food that people eat comes from large-scale industrial farms. The other 70 percent comes from small-scale farmers working on small plots of land.[3] Meanwhile, industrial agriculture accounts for 75 percent of the ecological damage being done to the planet.[4] These figures are routinely ignored, hidden, and denied, and the myth that industrial agriculture feeds the world is promoted worldwide.

A mechanized, violent paradigm shapes dominant views around the knowledge, science, technology, and policies for food and agriculture. In reality, a food system that destroys nature's economy—the ecological foundation on which food production rests—cannot feed the world. An agricultural system designed to displace small-scale farmers, who form the social foundation of real farming, cannot feed the world. Every aspect of industrial agriculture is rupturing the fragile web of life and destroying the foundations of food security.

Industrial agriculture is killing pollinators and friendly insects. Years ahead of his time, Einstein cautioned, "When the last bee disappears, humans will disappear." Today 75 percent of bee populations in some regions have been killed over the last three decades because of toxic pesticides.[5] Chemical pesticides kill beneficial insects and, in their place, create pests. Synthetic fertilizers destroy soil fertility by killing soil organisms that naturally create living soil, and in turn, contribute to soil erosion and soil degradation.

Industrial agriculture mines and pollutes water. Seventy percent of the water on the planet is being depleted and polluted by the intensive irrigation that is required in chemical-intensive industrial agriculture.[6] The nitrates in water from industrial farms are creating "dead zones" in the oceans: spaces where no life can exist.

Industrial agriculture is primarily a fossil-fuel-driven agriculture. Replacing people with fossil fuels has been made to look efficient under a logic that treats people as raw material or farming inputs. But the financial and ecological costs of fossil fuels are astronomical. In US agriculture, each worker has more than 250 hidden energy slaves behind her. An energy slave is the fossil-fuel equivalent to a person, and if we take into account the fossil-fuel intensity of our food production and consumption systems, it is all too clear that industrial agriculture consumes more than it produces. As Amory Lovins pointed out, "In terms of workforce, the population of the earth is not 4 billion but about 200 billion, the important point being that about 98 percent of them do not eat conventional food."[7] That is because they're not people; they're energy slaves, and they eat oil. Industrial agriculture uses ten units of fossil-fuel energy as an input to produce one unit of food as an output. The wasted energy goes toward polluting the atmosphere and destabilizing our climate.

The industrial paradigm of agriculture is causing climate change. Forty percent of all greenhouse gas emissions responsible for climate change come from a fossil-fuel-based global system of agriculture.[8] The fossil fuels used to make fertilizers, run farm machinery, and wastefully move food thousands of miles across the globe contribute to carbon dioxide emissions. Chemical nitrogen fertilizers emit nitrous oxide, which is 300 percent more destabilizing for the climate than carbon dioxide.[9] Additionally, factory farming is a major source of methane, another toxin responsible for global warming. In 1995 the United Nations calculated that industrial agriculture had pushed more than 75 percent of agro-biodiversity—the biodiversity found in agriculture—to extinction. Today, the number is likely to have reached 90 percent.

Paradoxically, while this ecological destruction of natural capital is justified in terms of "feeding people," the problem of hunger has grown. One billion people are permanently hungry, and another two billion suffer from food-related diseases like obesity. These conditions are two sides of the same coin: a nutrition crisis. As the McDonaldization of food spreads processed junk food across the globe, even those who do get enough to eat are rarely getting the nutrients they need. Contrary to popular belief, obesity isn't about rich people eating too much: it's often the poor in developing countries who bear the harshest brunt of diet-related diseases. Additionally, diseases linked to an industrial diet and poisons in our food, including cancer, are steadily growing. Commodities don't feed people; food does.

Even though the corporate industrial agriculture system creates hunger, even though it contributes only 25 percent to the food system while using 75 percent of the Earth's resources, and even though it is a dominant force of ecological destruction and a disruption of the natural systems on which food production depends, the myth that industrial agriculture feeds the world continues to be perpetuated. This myth is constructed on the basis of an obsolete paradigm, one that has, in fact, been discarded by science. False ideas of nature as dead matter and as something that can be manipulated at will by humans have allowed us to think that the more poisons we put into the food system, the more food we will grow. An ecologically destructive and nutritionally inefficient food system has become the dominant paradigm in our minds and the most touted practice on our lands, even though, in reality, small, biodiverse farms working with nature's processes produce most of the food we eat.

Industrial agriculture is intolerant of diversity. Diversity is nourishing and naturally resistant, but in order to increase profits, industrial agriculture makes crops dependent on external inputs such as chemical fertilizers, pesticides, herbicides, and genetically modified seeds. Not only does industrial agriculture look more and more like chemical warfare against the planet, the distribution of food also looks like war, with so-called "free trade" treaties pitting farmer against farmer, and country against country, in perpetual "competition" and conflict. "Free trade" allows corporations and investors to grab every seed, every drop of water, and every inch of land; it limitlessly exploits the Earth, the farmers, and all citizens. This model sees profits as the endgame, where no thought or care is given for the soil, for producers, and for people's health. Corporations do not grow food; they grow profits.

The industrial paradigm replaces truths with manipulation, and reality with fictions. The first fiction is the fiction of the corporation as a person. Acting under this guise of personhood, corporations write the rules of production and trade to maximize their profits and exploit living beings. A second fiction is that "capital"—not the ecological processes of nature and the hard and intelligent work of farmers—creates wealth and food. People and nature are reduced to mere inputs. The third fiction is that a system that uses more inputs than it produces is efficient and productive. This is manipulated by hiding the financial costs of fossil fuels and chemicals, as well as the devastating health and environmental costs of a chemical-intensive system to the planet and its people. A fourth fiction is that which is profitable to corporations is profitable and good for farmers. Actually, as the profits of corporations in food and agricultural systems grow, farmers become poorer by getting deeper in debt and are finally forced off their land. The fifth fiction is that food is a commodity. The reality is that the more food is converted into a commodity, the more it is taken from the poor, which creates hunger, and the more it is degraded in quality, which leads to disease.

What we are talking about here is not a food system—it is anti-food. Food comes into conflict with itself as it is violently pulled out of the food web and local economies to then be traded for profit and thrown away as waste. The result is ecological catastrophe, poverty, and hunger. The future of food depends on remembering that the web of life is a food web. This book is dedicated to this remembering, because forgetting the ecology of food is a recipe for famine and extinction.

Over the past three decades I have realized that our current food system is broken. In 1984 I began studying the Green Revolution in Punjab. The Green Revolution is the misleading name given to a chemical-based agricultural model that was introduced to India in 1965. Following World War II, chemical companies and factories were searching desperately for new markets for synthetic fertilizers made in the explosives factories of the war. Indigenous varieties of crops rejected the artificial fertilizers, so plants were redesigned as dwarf varieties to allow them to take up—and become dependent upon—chemicals. By the mid-1960s, this new seed/chemical package was ready to be exported to countries in the Global South under the label of the Green Revolution.

The false narrative perpetuated by the Green Revolution is essential to understanding the dominant narrative that has been created around food and agriculture. This narrative credits the Green Revolution with pulling India out of starvation, for which Norman Borlaug—the leading scientist on the project—was awarded the Nobel Peace Prize in 1970. But there was no starvation in India in 1965. Food prices had risen in cities due to a nationwide drought, and the country needed to import food grains. But under a policy to promote chemicals in agriculture, a condition was created by the US government and the World Bank under which food grains would be sent to India by America *only* if it also imported seeds and chemicals.

There was a huge gap between the Green Revolution's narrative of success and the realities in Punjab. Reduced to a land of rice and wheat, Punjab began producing *less* food and nutrition as a result of industrial agriculture. Once farmers in Punjab grew forty-one varieties of wheat, thirty-seven varieties of rice, four varieties of maize, eight varieties of *bajra,* sixteen varieties of sugarcane, nineteen varieties of pulses, and nine varieties of oilseeds.[10] The majority of this diversity was destroyed. In the place of wheat grains with names like Sharbati, Darra, Lal Pissi, and Malwa, which described the origins and quality of the crops, we find personality-less monocultures named HD 2329, PBW 343, and WH 542: crops infested with pests and diseases, requiring ever-higher doses of pesticides.

While the Green Revolution in Punjab has left behind desertified soils, depleted aquifers, disappearing biodiversity, indebted farmers, and a "cancer train" that carries the victims of pesticide-related cancer to Rajasthan for free treatment, this nonsustainable model is being exported to the eastern states of India and to Africa. Bill Gates, with his billions of dollars, is blindly pushing chemicals and commercial seeds into Africa through the Alliance for a Green Revolution in Africa. In fact, all world aid routed through policies of the G8 countries is undemocratically imposing a failed model on Africa. Sadly, the true lessons from Punjab's Green Revolution were only learned by those who were destroyed in its wake.

Today there is a second Green Revolution under way: one driven by GMOs. GMOs, or genetically modified organisms, are genetically engineered crops with genes for toxins introduced into them. Like the original Green Revolution, GMOs claim to "feed the world." But the reality is that GMOs do not produce more, they have led to increased chemical use, and they fail to control weeds and pests. Genetic engineering creates an entirely new type of pollution on our planet, negatively impacting plants and animals, human health, and the livelihoods of farmers and local communities. The only beneficiaries of GM crops are corporations, because they sell more toxic chemicals and they also collect royalties on seed. As a matter of fact, corporations' greed and desire to own seeds is the *only* reason why GMOs are being pushed undemocratically into food and farming systems across the world.

But something is shifting. The anger that burst in Punjab in 1984 is bursting everywhere—whether it be the streets of Egypt, where the Arab Spring began as protests against rising prices of bread; or Syria, where the conflict started as protests by peasants seeking relief for crop failure due to an intense drought; or millions of people from every walk of life joining the March against Monsanto, a self-organizing global citizens' movement protesting the control of corporations over what we grow and eat. There is discontent everywhere because the dominant industrialized and globalized food system, controlled by a handful of corporations, is destroying the planet, farmers' livelihoods, people's health, democracy, and peace. In the face of this, redesigning the food system has become a survival imperative.

So what is preventing us from transitioning to an ecologically friendly, people-friendly food system?

The first barrier comes from the power of corporations, which are rooted in the architecture of war. Just five seed and chemical giants—Monsanto, Syngenta, Bayer, Dow, and DuPont—seek to completely dominate our food system. Corporations are a legal construct that are now claiming personhood. But corporations are not people. They are not born and they do not die. They cannot grow food and they cannot eat food. Yet they are taking over our sustainable and nourishing food systems, replacing them with commodities and violence.

The second barrier comes from the militarized, mechanistic, reductionist, and fragmented paradigm of agriculture that creates a blindness to the contributions of diverse species and the ecological processes and functions that they provide and participate in. This paradigm refuses to acknowledge and include women and small-scale farmers, who provide most of the world's food, and whose knowledge is vital to sustainable food production.

The third barrier comes from greed and a calculus of prosperity based on greed. The greed of corporations for profits is blocking a transition to a healthy, sustainable, and democratic food system. For farmers, the system of corporate greed manifests in an imperative to chase an illusion of more money, even though farmers are the losers in a high-cost industrial system of production. As citizens, corporate greed reduces us to mere consumers, and the majority of us remain unaware of how, where, and by whom our food was grown, and what our food actually contains.

So who, then, *really* feeds the world? Again, we must ask ourselves what we mean by "food" and what we mean by "world." If "food" is the web of life—the currency of life, our nourishment, our cells, our blood, our mind, our culture, and our identity—and the "world" is Gaia—our rich and living planet, our Mother Earth, vibrant with diverse beings and ecosystems, multitudes of peoples and cultures—then it is the contributions of biodiversity, compassion, and the knowledge and intelligence of small-scale farmers that feed the world. My own research and lived experience over the last three decades has taught me that the answer to the food question does not lie in industrial agriculture but in agroecology and ecological farming.

Food is produced by the soil, the seed, the sun, the water, and the farmer, all interacting with one another. Food embodies ecological relationships, and the knowledge and science of the interactions and interconnectedness that produce food are called agroecology. **Agroecology feeds us.**

Fertile soil is the basis of food production. Soil fertility is created by billions of soil organisms that come together to form the soil food web. Biodiversity and soils rich in organic matter are also the best strategy for climate adaptation and water conservation. Water is vital for living soils, and organic farming conserves water by increasing the water-holding capacity of soils through recycling organic matter. The soil becomes like a sponge, which can absorb more water, thus reducing water use and also contributing to resilience to climate change. **Living soil feeds us.**

Pollinators like butterflies take pollen from one plant to another, fertilizing them in the process. Without pollinators, plants would not reproduce. **Pollinators feed us.**

Feeding the planet means sustaining the integrity and diversity of the food web: from the soil to the oceans, from microorganisms to mammals, from plants to humans. The food system is not outside nature and the Earth. It is based on the ecological processes through which the planet creates, maintains, and renews life. The planet is living: its currency is life; its currency is food. As the ancient Indian text *Taittiriya Upanishad* reminds us, "Everything is food. Everything is something else's food." Nature, contrary to what industrial agriculture tells us, is very much *alive,* and its **diversity feeds us.**

Farmers are plant breeders and seed savers, soil conservators and soil builders, water preservers and water keepers. Farmers are food producers. While using only 30 percent of the world's resources, small-scale farmers provide 70 percent of the planet's food. **Small-scale farmers, farming families, and gardeners feed us.**

Seed is the first link in the food system. Without seed there is no food. Without diversity of seed, there is no diversity of food and nutrition, which is vital to health. Without diversity of seed, there is no climate resilience in times of climate chaos and climate instability. **Seeds feed us.**

Food is not a commodity; it is not a perfume or a piece of jewelry that can be sold anywhere in the world. Every being engages with food differently, and each culture or locality produces its own food. Since everyone must eat, local food sovereignty is the key to food security: **localization feeds us.**

Working with seed, biodiversity, soil, and water, according to the laws of nature and ecology, is the basis of food production. This knowledge and its practice have traditionally belonged to women, who make up the majority of the world's food producers. **Women feed us.**

Food is life, and it is created through living processes that sustain life. In agriculture and food production, nature and nature's laws come first. Violating these laws and trespassing on nature's limits of renewal—of seed and soil, water and energy—is a recipe for food insecurity and future famines. While rejuvenating nature's economy, ecological agriculture produces more and better food, and it rejuvenates the health and well-being of communities. Taking care of the Earth and feeding people go hand in hand.

Feeding the planet raises some of the most fundamental questions of our times. The food question becomes an ethical question about our relationship with the Earth and other species; about whether we have the right to push species to extinction or deny large numbers of the human family safe, healthy, and nutritious food. It becomes an ecological question about whether humans will live as members of the Earth Community or will push themselves to extinction by destroying the ecological foundations of agriculture. It becomes a cultural question about our food cultures, our identity, and our sense of place and rootedness.

Feeding people is a knowledge question about whether we continue to think through a destructive, reductionist, mechanistic paradigm, viewing seed and soil as dead matter and mere machines to be manipulated and poisoned, or whether we think of seed and soil as living, self-organizing, self-renewing systems that can give us food without the use of chemicals and poisons. It is also a knowledge question about whether we see centuries of farming by peasants as based on knowledge, and farmers as intelligent, or whether we think of farmers as ignorant just because they may not have been to college.

The food question is also an economic question: about whether the poor eat or go hungry; about whether public taxes go to subsidize an unhealthy and nonsustainable food system; about whether seeds are in the commons or owned through patents by corporations; and about whether food is distributed on principles of justice, fairness, and sovereignty, or on the basis of the unfair rules of so-called "free trade."

Once I realized how misguided and false the dominant system of agriculture was, I dedicated my life to saving seeds and promoting organic farming and ecological agriculture. Instead of intensifying chemical and capital inputs that were pushing our small-scale farmers into debt, I committed myself to intensifying biodiversity and ecological processes, working with nature, rather than declaring war against her.

In 1987 I started Navdanya, a movement for saving seeds, protecting biodiversity, and spreading ecological methods of farming. We have helped create more than one hundred community seed banks, which have provided open access seeds to farmers to grow tasty, nutritious crops with no external inputs, thus increasing their own nutrition while also increasing their incomes. These seed banks have rescued farmers in times of climate extremes, including droughts, floods, and cyclones. Beginning with the saving and sharing of seed, we now share the seeds of the knowledge of agroecology. Through our Earth University we spread the ideas and practices related to living seed, living soil, living food, living economies, and living democracies. Through the practice of biodiversity-based, ecological agriculture, we teach how food can be grown in health and abundance, and farming can be done to enhance the fertility of the soil, increase biodiversity, conserve water, and reduce greenhouse gases that contribute to climate change.

The contest between the two paradigms of food is a contest between two ideas and organizing principles. One paradigm is based on the Law of Exploitation and the Law of Domination, beginning with wars and rooted in violence. The second paradigm is embedded in agroecology and living economies and is based on the Law of Return: of giving back to society, small-scale farmers, and the Earth. It embodies the values of sharing and caring, not selfishness and greed. Today, a paradigm shift has become a global survival imperative that cannot wait any longer.

Who Really *Feeds the World?* is a distillation of three decades of research and action, and a call for a global shift.

We need a paradigm shift and a power shift. Industrial agriculture shaped by corporate greed does not, and cannot, bring us sustainability and health. Instead, we can make the transition to agroecology and feed ourselves in abundance by focusing on saving seeds, giving back to the soil, nurturing biodiversity, and protecting our small-scale farmers and women. We must stop impoverishing our beautiful planet. It is in our hands to sow the seeds of hope for a food system that works for the health and well-being of the planet and all its people.

1

Agroecology Feeds the World,
Not a Violent Knowledge Paradigm

Over the last ten thousand years, humanity has farmed ecologically. Systems and cycles of nature have given rise to renewal, reproduction, and diversity, allowing all beings to peacefully coexist. These sustainable systems are not stagnant or static; they are in constant evolution. Within these ecological systems, organic farming has thrived. In fact, it thrived so well that even those who first stood to profit from industrial agriculture found that there was little their chemicals and pesticides could do to "improve" traditional ecological farming.

As early as 1889, Dr. John Augustus Voelcker was sent to India to advise the imperial British government on the application of chemical agriculture to India's farms. On studying Indian farming systems, Voelcker stated, "there is little or nothing that can be improved.... Certain it is that I, at least, have never seen a more perfect picture of careful cultivation. I may be bold to say that it is a much easier task to propose improvements in English agriculture than to make valuable suggestions for that of India."[1]

More than twenty years later, Sir Albert Howard, the "father" of modern sustainable farming, wrote of India and China: "The agricultural practices of the Orient have passed the supreme test, they are almost as permanent as those of the primeval forest, of the prairie, or of the ocean."[2] What is remarkable about these statements is that these two men were, after all, colonizers, looking for larger profits from and stronger control over indigenous land. And even they could find no deficiencies within such "perfect" systems of cultivation. Contrary to commonly held opinion, famines at the time took place not because indigenous agricultural systems did not produce abundant food, but because of colonial exploitation, as is evidenced by the Great Bengal famine of 1943.[3]

In the last fifty years, however, something has shifted. The last half century has been a short-lived experiment with nonsustainable, chemical-intensive, water-intensive, and capital-intensive agriculture.[4] This new farming, often incorrectly touted as "conventional," has destroyed the ecological foundations of agriculture, devastated natural environments, and resulted in food insecurity across the world. Given that self-sustaining systems have been in existence for millennia, how did this ecologically devastating farming become the dominant paradigm for approaching agriculture the world over? To answer this question, we must look at the ways of thinking—the knowledge paradigms—that gave rise to this new agriculture.

As physicist Thomas Kuhn has written, all scientific systems are framed by knowledge paradigms. This is also true for the science and technology used in agriculture. Technological tools for food production do not exist independently of the knowledge paradigm of which they are a part, and the sophistication and sustainability of an agricultural farming system is dependent on the sophistication of the knowledge paradigm that governs it.

Traditional agriculture and organic farming have their roots in several strands of knowledge, which are collectively recognized as the emerging knowledge paradigm of agroecology. Agroecology takes into account the interconnectedness of life and the complex processes that take place within nature. The time-tested agroecological knowledge of centuries, evolved in diverse ecosystems and cultures, is now being reinforced by the latest findings in modern science. There is new scientific knowledge in epigenetics about the interaction between genes and the environment, new knowledge of the ecological services provided by biodiversity and ecosystems, and a scientific recognition of the fact that the Earth is living. These are all contributing to the emergence of agroecology as a widely recognized scientific paradigm.

During the industrial agriculture revolution, these traditional knowledge systems were replaced by a militarized way of thinking that promoted violence toward the Earth. The tools designed under this system were devised in ignorance of the fragile web of life, and they went on to disrupt and destroy the ecological foundations of food production. Industrial agriculture is not a knowledge system based on the understanding of ecological processes within an agroecosystem; rather, it is a collection of violent tools. These tools were very literally the products of warfare and relied on agrochemicals that were originally designed to kill people.

The discussion about who really feeds the world is first and foremost a discussion about which knowledge paradigm is a better guarantee for sustainable food production. Sophisticated, sustainable systems of both thought and food production have always existed. Humanity, after all, did not start eating in contemporary times. How then did we arrive at a situation where the Green Revolution and industrial agriculture displaced and destroyed systems that have nourished humanity over millennia and substituted the knowledge of ecological agricultural systems—agroecology—with the tools of warfare? And how did an outmoded mechanistic philosophy continue to dominate agriculture, even as emerging scientific disciplines converged with indigenous knowledge to create a system view of farming and food? And, finally, how can we move into a future based on the ecological foundations of agriculture, without which food production cannot take place?

When poisons are introduced into agriculture to control pests, or when GMOs are introduced under the argument of "feeding the world," the justification given is always "science." But "science" does not have a singular entity, and it did not come into existence within a vacuum. Today, what we generally refer to as "science" is in fact Western, mechanistic, reductionist modern science, which became the dominant practice of understanding the world during the Industrial Revolution and has continued as the dominant paradigm.

Beginning in the mid-1700s when colonialism was at its peak, land that was once shared by communities, called the commons, needed to be enclosed in order to build industries and empires. To do this, the knowledge of the Earth and its species as interconnected and mutually beneficial needed to be replaced by something that allowed violence toward the land. To shape the industrial system in the form of new, violent technologies, and to shape the capitalist system in the form of a new, profit-driven economics, a certain *type* of science was promoted and privileged as the *only* scientific knowledge system. Two scientific theories came to dominate this new, industrial paradigm, and they continue to shape practices of food, agriculture, health, and nutrition even today.

The first is a Newtonian-Cartesian idea of separation: a fragmented world made of fixed, immutable atoms. In this worldview, as Newton himself writes, the "solid, massy, impenetrable, moveable particles ... are so very hard, as never to wear, or break in pieces: no ordinary power being able to divide, what God himself made one in the first creation.... And therefore, that Nature may be lasting."[5] This understanding of the world sees nature as composed of dead matter: a Lego set where immutable particles and pieces can be used, moved, and substituted without any overarching consequences. This mechanistic assumption has today given rise to genetic reductionism and genetic determinism, and has led to the development of what has come to be known as the central dogma of molecular biology, which is the belief that genetic material, or DNA, serves as a master molecule. This dogma was so fundamentally inscribed into scientific belief that it was "the equivalent of science's Ten Commandments, written in stone."[6]

Subsequently, this belief system has provided the basis for genetic engineering and genetically modified seeds, or GMOs. As we will see throughout this book, instead of killing pests and growing food, GMOs have reduced food production while producing new superpests and superweeds, which are growing increasingly tolerant to the sprays meant to kill them. And like the scientific paradigm that gave rise to them, GMOs have displaced indigenous knowledge, and in particular, women's knowledge, with a mechanized, reductive worldview. As geneticist Dr. Mae-Wan Ho puts it, "The organism is doing its own natural genetic modification with great finesse, a molecular dance of life that's necessary for survival. Unfortunately, genetic engineers do not know the steps or the rhythm and music of the dance."[7]

Newtonian-Cartesian theories have been proved to be false by new sciences such as quantum theory, ecology, the new biology, and epigenetics. Quantum theory teaches us that the world is not made of hard, immutable matter but of fields of potential with a dynamic transformation of particles into waves and waves into particles. My doctoral thesis on the foundations of quantum theory focused on inseparability, not Newtonian separation, as the defining characteristic of a quantum universe. Ecology teaches us that everything is a web of life and that Gaia is a self-organizing system at every level, from the cell to the organism to the planet. Epigenetics teaches us that the idea that there are atoms of life called "genes"—which determine the traits of all living organisms—is not true. It shows us that the environment influences genes, and genes do not regulate or organize themselves independently of their surroundings.

In *The Doctrine of DNA,* Richard Lewontin writes:

> DNA is a dead molecule, among the more nonreactive, chemically inert molecules in the world. It has no power to reproduce itself.

Rather, it is produced out of elementary materials by a complex cellular machinery of proteins.... While it is often said that DNA produces proteins, in fact proteins (enzymes) produce DNA. When we refer to genes as self-replicating, we endow them with a mysterious, autonomous power that seems to place them above ordinary materials of the body. Yet if anything in the world can be said to be self-replicating, it is not the gene, but the entire organism as a complex system.[8]

The second significant theory that has framed the knowledge paradigm for industrial agriculture is Darwin's theory of competition as the basis for evolution. In his book *The Biology of Belief,* Bruce H. Lipton writes:

[Darwin] concluded that living organisms are perpetually embroiled in a struggle for existence. For Darwin, struggle and violence are not only a part of animal nature, but the principal forces behind evolutionary involvement. In the final chapter of *The Origin of Species: By Means of Natural Selection, or, The Preservation of Favoured Races in the Struggle for Life,* Darwin wrote of an inevitable "struggle for life" and that evolution was driven by "the way of nature, from famine and death."[9]

But life does not evolve through competition; rather, life evolves through cooperation and self-organization. Fifty trillion cells cooperate to create the human body. Millions of species cooperate to shape ecosystems and the planet.

The Darwinian paradigm of competition has fueled the industrial agriculture paradigm. Monocultures are born of the idea that plants compete with each other, when the reality is that plants cooperate with each other. In the mixed farming system of corn, beans, and squash in Mexico, for example, nitrogen-fixing beans and pulses provide free nitrogen to cereals, and in return, the stalks of cereals like maize or millets provide support for the bean stalks to climb. In turn, the squash provides cover to the soil, preventing soil erosion, water evaporation, and the emergence of weeds. Together, these diverse crops provide nutrition for soil, animals, and human beings. The Darwinian paradigm, on the other hand, sees every insect as being at war with humans, and therefore as something to be exterminated with poisons.

Together, these two scientific theories form a reductionist, mechanistic paradigm of knowledge that permits limitless exploitation. While the tools of implementation under this paradigm vary, the privileging of this knowledge has provided the intellectual foundation for industrialism as a system of production and of control over nature. Under the industrial systems of agriculture born from this paradigm, soil is treated as an inert container for chemical fertilizers, plants are defined as factories, and seeds are seen as machines that run on agrochemicals.

The Newtonian-Cartesian theory of fragmentation and separation, and the Darwinian paradigm of competition, have led to a nonrenewable use of the Earth's resources, a nonsustainable model of food and agriculture, and an unhealthy model of health and nutrition. An emphasis on the legitimacy of these arguments as the sole "scientific" approach has created a knowledge apartheid by discounting the knowledge of farmers and the intelligence and creativity of Mother Earth. After all, if nature is already dead, how can you kill her?

––––––––––

The scientific paradigms of violence paved the road for intensified warfare. During World War II, large companies made even larger sums of money from the deaths of millions of people. After the wars ended, an industry that grew and made profits by making explosives and chemicals for war, including for concentration camps, remodeled itself as the agrochemical industry. Faced with the choice of closing down or "rebranding," explosives factories started to make synthetic fertilizers, and war chemicals began to be used as pesticides and herbicides. At the heart of industrial agriculture is the use of poisons; the system of industrial agriculture is a necroeconomy—its profits are rooted in death and destruction.

The chemical push changed how agriculture was both understood and lived. Instead of working with ecological processes and taking the well-being and health of the entire agroecosystem into account, agriculture was reduced to an external input system based on poisons. So where once there was a farming system in which everything was internally recycled and reused, from the soil to the water to the plants, there was now a system that relied on external inputs of seeds, chemicals, and fertilizers that constantly needed to be purchased.

Industrial farming is a massive contributor to climate change. It is responsible for 25 percent of the world's carbon dioxide emissions, 60 percent of methane gas emissions, and 80 percent of nitrous oxide, which are all powerful greenhouse gases. As we shall see in the following chapters, it has also contributed to soil erosion and infertility, water pollution and aquifer depletion, and the destruction of self-sufficient societies across the world.

Even though small farms produce more food through diversity, agriculture has become focused on large, monoculture farms based on the intensive use of chemicals, fossil fuels, and capital. Instead of diverse food for people of diverse cultures based on more than 8,500 plant species across the world, these farms produce monocultures of a handful of commodities to be traded globally. Monocultures based on external inputs—such as chemical fertilizers and pesticides—are also more vulnerable to pests, and they fare poorly compared to a diverse, organic farming system. The shift from diversity to monocultures in farming has led to a shift from diversity to monocultures in diets. These agricultural shifts impoverished both the health of soil and the health of people. War, as we all know, is never an undertaking for health or for life.

Under a reductionist knowledge paradigm, the effects of war on agriculture led to a reductionist economics that privileged commodity production. Commodity production is to economics what fragmented thinking is to biology. The same system that sees genes as master molecules deems commodities to be the master currency of the world. The system for managing commodities is gross domestic product, or GDP. But GDP did not always exist. In fact, it was created in order to finance war, so that governments could justify pulling out resources from sustenance to fund warfare. GDP is dangerous to agriculture because it has resulted in the fictitious idea that if you produce what you consume, you do not produce.[10] So where you once had both nature and women as key producers of food, you now have commodities—that which creates economic profit—being counted as production.

Through this artificially imposed economy, society has been reduced to producers and consumers of commodities, rather than growers and eaters of food. Nature's production of ecological goods and services, and the ability of societies to maintain nature and provide sustenance, were first erased in people's minds and then in real ecosystems and local economies. This erasure of centuries-old knowledge that provides nourishment and sustenance to soil and society is the basis of ecological destruction and leads to poverty and hunger across the world.

The construction of the reductionist economic paradigm gave mysterious qualities to capital and to corporations as the creative forces that bring us food. By rendering invisible the production carried out by nature, women, and small-scale farmers, the only part of the food economy made visible was that which was under corporate control. Systems based on diversity were replaced by monocultures, which produced less nutrition but more commodities. Farmers were made dependent on purchasing costly seeds and chemicals, and many debt-trapped farmers were eventually driven to suicide.

———————

Within an agroecological system that sustains life, there are three coexisting economies: nature's economy, people's economy, and the market economy. Together they make up an economy of sustainability. Nature's economy includes biodiversity, soil fertility, and water conservation, which together provide the ecological foundations on which agriculture depends. People's economy is an economy of sustenance, where communities produce what is needed and look after each other. And finally, the market economy involves exchanges and interactions between real human beings, not corporations.

The sustainability of both nature's economy and people's economy is based on the Law of Return: of giving back to seeds, soil, and society.

9

The Law of Return of the seed sustains the cycle of living seed. It includes allowing seed to turn into seed while also giving us food. It also allows for living seed evolved by nature and farmers to move freely from farmer to farmer through what we call seed freedom. The Law of Return of the soil includes giving back organic matter to the soil, to renew fertility and sustain living soils. The Law of Return in society includes giving back to farmers their fair share for producing food and sustaining us with nourishment, so they can live a life of dignity and freedom. It includes cooperation and mutuality as well as closing the cycle between production and consumption. And above all, it includes the Law of Return between generations, with each generation remembering the gifts received from our ancestors, and leaving behind a legacy of seed, soil, knowledge, and culture for generations to come.

In a sustainable system, these three economies exist as a stable pyramid. Nature's economy, in all her plentiful, renewing sustenance, forms the large base of the pyramid. Nature's economy supports people's economy, which helps recycle and renew the natural resources it uses. The tip of the pyramid is then the market economy based on nature's and people's economy, which is made up of the interactions of different communities to share resources, knowledge, and ideas.

But under the reductionist, mechanistic paradigm of knowledge and profits, the idea of sustainability itself is being mutated. There are quite clearly two different meanings of "sustainability." The real meaning refers to nature and people's sustainability, and it recognizes that nature supports our lives and livelihoods and is the primary source of sustenance. Sustaining nature implies maintaining the integrity of nature's processes, cycles, and rhythms.

Now, however, there is a second kind of "sustainability," one that refers to the Market with a capital "M." This paradigm only measures growth in the Market economy through GDP, even though this growth is often associated with destruction and shrinkage of nature's economy and people's economy. Sustainability in this all-powerful Market involves ensuring supplies of raw material, flow of commodities, accumulation of capital, and returns on investment. It cannot provide the sustenance that we are already losing by impairing nature's capacities to support life. The growth of global markets hides the destruction of the local economy of domestic production and consumption. And since industrial raw materials and market commodities can be substituted—whereas people and nature can't—sustainability is translated into the substitutability of materials, which is further translated into nature's convertibility into profits and cash.

This mutated idea of sustainability has turned the economic pyramid on its head, making it ecologically and socially unstable. At the top is a large, profit-driven Market; below is a smaller, also market-driven people's economy; and finally, nature's economy is reduced to a tiny tip, attempting to hold up a system that only takes and never gives back.

We need to restore the pyramid to its original, enduring form. This transition to sustainable living agriculture requires that the two neglected economies of nature and people should be made visible in the assessment of productivity and cost-benefit analysis in agriculture. Sustainability criteria can be internalized in agriculture only when nature's economy reflects the health of nature's ecological processes—the health of soil, the health of biodiversity, the health of water systems—and when people's economy reflects the real health of people's socioeconomic and nutritional status. In order to begin this reversal, we must first reverse the dominant knowledge paradigms that have framed these debates.

The knowledge of conservation has never been recognized as knowledge by the gatekeepers of reductionist science and economics. Instead, the dominant paradigms of knowledge have been focused on exploitation. Take, for example, the knowledge behind certain types of forestry. A tree on its own has no value; it is only when you cut the tree that the value is accrued. Under this logic, the only knowledge that matters is the knowledge that feeds the market. But the tree provides shade, gives fruit, sustains soil, birds, and animals, and provides the oxygen that we breathe. This is the knowledge that the emerging field of agroecology reclaims.

Agroecology is the new name given to the scientific paradigm that covers all ancient, sustainable, and traditional farming systems that were based on ecological principles. These practices were usually only explained in traditional, localized worldviews, such as knowledge passed down from generation to generation in tribal and indigenous communities. Agroecology takes all of this diversity, combines it with knowledge from new sciences like epigenetics and quantum theory that reinforce the connectedness of the world, and produces a new, sustainable knowledge paradigm.

The paradigm of agroecological knowledge reshapes the ways in which we understand issues surrounding food and agriculture.

- It recognizes interconnections in nature and is based on the application of ecological science to food and agricultural systems, instead of a reductionist, mechanistic, and militarized approach.
- It promotes the health of soil, plants, animals, and human beings.
- It enhances the ecological integrity of food production through the Law of Return.
- It conserves biodiversity and intensifies biodiversity services such as pollinators, rendering agrochemical inputs such as pesticides redundant.
- It maximizes "health per acre" and "nutrition per acre" instead of "yield per acre."
- It is based on seed freedom, where the control of seeds lies with farmers, instead of a system that views seeds as corporate intellectual property.
- It creates the socioeconomic, political, and cultural context for the exercise of food freedom and food sovereignty.
- It is centered on women's knowledge of biodiversity, ecosystems, health, and nutrition, instead of corporate-controlled and -manipulated knowledge based on monocultures.
- It is based on a sense of place and gives priority to the local, instead of the unfair privilege given to global corporations.

Agroecology is a very real alternative to the broken, violent paradigm of industrial chemical agriculture. As we shall see in the following chapters, it is the methods and practices developed by agroecology that really feed the world. Where industrial agriculture destroys biodiversity, ecological agriculture conserves and rejuvenates diverse species. Where industrial agriculture depletes and pollutes water, organic farming conserves water by increasing the water-holding capacity of soils by recycling organic matter. Where industrial agriculture sees nature as dead matter, or as a machine, agroecology injects life back into the Earth, seeing her as a living, breathing being.

In the agroecological paradigm of knowledge, and in organic farming, food is the web of life. Humans are part of this web, as cocreators and coproducers, as well as eaters. When we save seed and replant it, we become part of the cycle of life. When we return organic matter to the soil, we are feeding the soil organisms. Working according to nature's laws is participating in nature's processes of creation and production. This is the basis of sustainability of food and agricultural systems. An agroecological knowledge system feeds the world, not a violent, reductionist paradigm of agriculture.

2

Living Soil Feeds the World, Not Chemical Fertilizers

Whatever I dig of you, O Earth,
May that grow quickly upon you,
O pure One, may my thrust never pierce thy
Vital points, Thy Heart

—"PRITHVI-SUKTA," A PRAYER IN THE ANCIENT INDIAN
TEXT ATHARVA VEDA[1]

English botanist Sir Albert Howard arrived in Indore, India, in 1905. There he began work with his wife Gabrielle as an agricultural adviser, observing the methods of cultivation used by peasants and farmers. Howard is known as the father of organic farming, but it was actually the peasants of India who fathered and mothered the scientist's now-famous agricultural philosophy and practice. It was here he began espousing farming techniques that returned nutrients to the soil, and in his several writings he most famously observed, "Health in soil, plant, animal, and man is one great subject."[2]

The soil is a living system, with billions of soil organisms weaving an intricate soil food web to create, maintain, and renew soil fertility.

All food production rests on this web. The well-being of the soil is vital to human well-being, and from this point of view, the aim of fertilization is not to simply increase yields and fertilize plants but to nurture living soil.

However, the reductionist paradigm that paved the way for industrial chemical agriculture treats soil as an inert, empty container for chemical fertilizers. After World War I, manufacturers of explosives whose factories were equipped for nitrogen fixation had to find other markets for their products. Synthetic fertilizers provided a convenient "conversion" for peaceful uses of war products,[3] except instead of being peaceful, these chemicals waged a battle against the soil and against the Earth. Following World War II, this war against the planet was led under the banner of the Green Revolution in a bid to export these toxic chemicals to the Global South.

In India alone, twenty years of Green Revolution agriculture have succeeded in destroying the fertility of Punjab's soils. These soils were maintained across centuries by generations of farming families and could have been indefinitely maintained if international "experts" and Indian followers had not mistakenly believed that technologies could substitute for land, and that chemicals could replace the organic fertility of soils.

Today, 24 billion metric tons of fertile soils are lost from world agricultural systems each year. India is losing 6.6 billion metric tons of soil per year, China is losing 5.5 billion metric tons, and the United States is losing 3 billion metric tons. In fact, soil is being lost at ten to forty times the rate at which it can be replenished naturally. Soil nutrients lost to erosion cost $20 billion annually. Chemical monocultures also make soils more vulnerable to drought and further contribute to food insecurity. Resulting from this degradation are reduced availability of clean water, and increased vulnerability of the affected areas to climate change, food insecurity, and poverty. Today, 1.5 billion people in all parts of the world are already directly affected by the loss of land through reduced income or food insecurity.[4] According to the current status of soil degradation, if we continue to destroy the living soil of our planet, there will be 30 percent less food on the planet over the next twenty to fifty years.[5]

Fueled by the Law of Exploitation and the Law of Domination, in the place of soils, we now have chemical fertilizers. The push for more fertilizers was an important factor in the spread of the new seeds, because wherever the new seeds went, they opened up new markets for chemical fertilizers. In 1967, at a meeting in New Delhi, Norman Borlaug—who is credited with the "success" of the Green Revolution in India—was emphatic about the role of fertilizers in the new agricultural order. "If I were a member of your parliament," he told the politicians and diplomats in the audience, "I would leap from my seat every fifteen minutes and yell at the top of my voice, 'Fertilizers! Give the farmers more fertilizers.' There is no more vital message in India than this. Fertilizers will give India more food."[6]

But no technology system can claim to feed the world while it destroys life in the soil. This is why the Green Revolution's claims—or genetic engineering's claims—that its technologies will feed the world are false. Intrinsic to these technologies are recipes for killing the life of the soil, thus accelerating soil erosion and degradation. Degraded and dead soils, soils without organic matter, soils without soil organisms, and soils with no water-holding capacity do not create food security; they create famines and are at the heart of the food crisis the world is facing today.

Healthy and fertile soils make healthy plants, which in turn make healthy people. Howard wrote:

> A soil teeming with healthy life in the shape of abundant microflora will bear healthy plants, and these, when consumed by animals and man, will confer health on animals and man. But an infertile soil, that is, one lacking sufficient microbial, fungus, and other life, will pass on some form of deficiency to the plant, and such plant, in turn, will pass on some form of deficiency to animals and man.[7]

The millions of organisms found in soil are the source of its fertility. The greatest biomass in soil consists of microorganisms. Soil microorganisms maintain soil structure, contribute to the biodegradation of dead plants and animals, and fix nitrogen. They are the key to soil fertility, and their destruction by chemicals threatens our survival and our food security. A 1997 Danish study analyzed a single cubic meter of soil and found thousands of small earthworms, fifty thousand insects and mites, and twelve million roundworms. A single gram of the soil contained thirty thousand protozoa, fifty thousand algae, four hundred thousand fungi, and billions of individual bacteria. It is this amazing biodiversity that maintains and rejuvenates soil fertility[8] and allows workers in the soil, or soil organisms, to flourish. These include fungi, bacteria, nematodes, and earthworms.

In uncontaminated soil, organic matter is broken down by soil organisms to form humus. *Humus* is the Latin word for "soil" or "earth." Humus is organic matter digested by soil organisms and made into living soil. One important characteristic of humus is that it functions as a sponge and can hold up to 90 percent of its weight in water. Soil that lacks humus is more vulnerable to drought, nutrient deficiency, and soil erosion.

Soils rich in humus are rich in fungi like mycorrhizae, which cannot exist without humus. Mycorrhizae create a symbiotic relationship with plants by entering the roots and mobilizing nutrients and moisture for plants. In a cycle of codependence, these fungi also contribute to forming humus and binding soil.

Living soils are teeming with beneficial bacteria. One teaspoon of soil has between one hundred million and one billion bacteria, which translates into one metric ton per every acre. Bacteria decompose and immobilize nutrients, which are retained in their cells, preventing soil nutrient loss. They produce substances that bind soil particles into aggregates—or compound soil particles—preventing soil erosion and increasing the water-holding capacity of soil.

Actinomycetes are bacteria that break down organic matter and live on humus to provide a glue to bind soil particles into aggregates. In the absence of soil microorganisms, soil does not bind. Instead, it becomes dust and is easily blown away by wind and washed away by water. Living soils also have nitrogen-fixing bacteria, which create a symbiotic relationship with the plant root and give the plant nitrogen in exchange for carbon.

Nematodes—or multicellular roundworms—get their name from the Greek word for "thread": *nema*. Ninety percent of nematodes reside in the top 15 cm of soil. Nematodes do not decompose organic matter but, instead, feed on living material. Nematodes can effectively regulate bacterial populations by eating up to five thousand bacteria per minute and, in the process, produce nitrogen.[9]

Earthworms are essential to living soils and soil fertility. In 1881, Darwin published a book entitled *The Formation of Vegetable Mould through the Action of Worms, with Observations on Their Habits.* Of worms, he wrote, "It may be doubted whether there are many other animals which have played so important a part in the history of creatures."[10] Earthworms are far more sophisticated than the most expensive fertilizer factories, because they not only provide fertility, they also increase the water-holding capacity and air volume of the soil, which are essential to living soil. Earthworms burrow through the soil to make small tunnels through which air and water can move. Earthworms increase the air volume of soil by up to 30 percent and the water-holding capacity of soil by 20 percent. This makes soil more resilient to drought. Soils with earthworms also drain ten times faster than those without, which makes soil resilient to floods. In a single square meter of organic soil, there can be anywhere from thirty to three hundred earthworms.

In addition to earthworms, fungi, and bacteria, between ten thousand and one hundred thousand green and blue algae cells are found per gram of soil. Between one thousand and one hundred thousand mites, spiders, ants, beetles, centipedes, and millipedes are found per square meter of organic soil. The more soil organisms present, the healthier the soil; it is more fertile, retains more water, and is less prone to erosion.

Nitrogen is an essential component of farming because it helps plants make their food. In order for nitrogen to be used, it must be "fixed" from the atmosphere in a process that converts it to ammonium. In factories, nitrogen is fixed from the air with huge amounts of fossil-fuel and energy use. In organic farming, where different plants grow side by side, nitrogen-fixing crops like pulses and legumes give us free nitrogen. These plants have a symbiotic relationship with rhizobia, which are bacteria in the soil that enter plant roots and help them access nitrogen from the air through biological nitrogen-fixing.

Additionally, in organic farming there are many plant species that give us natural green manure. Sesbania, glyricidia, and crotalaria, for example, can increase soil fertility immensely. These are usually grown as hedges in traditional agriculture, though they are nowhere to be seen in industrial monocultures. They are very effective, and glyricidia, as a hedge, can yield biomass or organic matter of up to 6–8 metric tons per hectare per year. Proponents of industrial agriculture repeatedly tell us that organic farming is not possible because there is not enough organic matter. But with green manures we can produce huge amounts of organic nitrogen and organic matter, which can replace the synthetic fertilizers that deplete soil fertility by killing soil organisms.

Ecological agriculture is based on recycling organic matter, and hence recycling nutrients. It is based on the Law of Return and on giving nutrients back to the soil, not simply taking nutrition out of it. Taking without giving is a robbery of the soil and a banditry, "a particularly mean form of banditry, because it involves the robbing of future generations which are not here to defend themselves."[11]

Sir Albert Howard writes in *An Agricultural Testament:*

> The feature of the manuring of the West is the use of artificial manures. The factories engaged during the Great War in the fixation of nitrogen for the manufacture of explosives had to find other markets, the use of nitrogenous fertilizers in agriculture increased, until today, the majority of farmers and market gardeners base their manorial programme on the cheapest forms of nitrogen (N), phosphorus

(P), and potassium (K) on the market. What may be conveniently described as the NPK mentality dominates farming in the experimental stations and in the countryside. Vested interests, entrenched in time[s] of national emergency, have gained a stronghold.[12]

In the industrial agriculture paradigm, soil is seen as dead matter: an empty container for pouring in synthetic fertilizers, especially NPK. This is done despite the fact that plants and soils need thirty-three elements for healthy growth. With their roots in war, these synthetic fertilizers continue war against our living soil.

Mycorrhizae bacteria and earthworms do not survive the application of chemical fertilizers. Fertilizers block the soil capillaries, which supply nutrients and water to plants. Infiltration of rain is stopped, runoff increases, and soil faces droughts, requiring ever-increasing irrigation and ever-increasing fossil fuels for pumping groundwater.

About two-thirds of the nitrogen fertilizer applied is not taken up by the plant; instead, it contaminates groundwater with nitrate pollution. It also contaminates surface waters, leading to eutrophication (overfertilization) of rivers and lakes, and creates dead zones in coastal waters. Large parts of nitrogen fertilizer escape into the air as nitrous oxide, which has an atmospheric life of 166 years and is three hundred times more damaging to the atmosphere as carbon dioxide. In spite of what the chemical companies would like us to believe, the reality is that nitrogen-fixing crops can provide enough nitrogen to substitute for synthetic nitrogen. Ecological alternatives that create, maintain, and rejuvenate living soils do so at zero cost, and are much more effective in increasing soil fertility and agricultural fertility than industrial fertilizers.

While destroying the sources of soil fertility and destabilizing the climate, synthetic fertilizers also waste financial resources through high costs and public subsidies. The global annual consumption of fertilizers is 164.4 million metric tons, which consist of 105 metric tons of nitrogen, 37.9 metric tons of phosphorous, and 21.5 metric tons of potash.[13] On the other hand, earthworm castings—what earthworms excrete into the soil—can amount to up to 36 metric tons per acre per year, contain three times more exchangeable nitrogen, seven times more phosphorous, three times more exchangeable magnesium, eleven times more potash, and one and one-half times more calcium than artificially fertilized soil.

Synthetic fertilizers use natural gas, so the manufacturing of synthetic fertilizers is a highly energy-intensive process. One kg of nitrogen fertilizer requires the energy equivalent of two liters of diesel. One kg of phosphate fertilizer requires the energy equivalent of half a liter of diesel. In 2000, the energy consumed while manufacturing fertilizers across the world was equivalent to 191 *billion* liters of diesel. This number is projected to rise to 277 billion by 2030.[14] While industrial agriculture claims to have reduced the amount of labor required, all it has done is replace the hard work of people with invisible "energy slaves"—the fossil-fuel equivalent of the work of a human being—and thus increase the ecological footprint of farming.

Today we are living in the age of "peak oil," which is M. King Hubbert's term for the point at which the planet reaches the highest possible level of oil production. After this, oil production will necessarily decrease.[15] Decreasing production will mean increasing prices, and the unprecedented increase in the price of oil since 2008 is a sign of an emerging crisis. As Heinberg put it, "The party's over."

Since synthetic nitrogen is based on fossil fuels, prices of fertilizers also go up when the price of oil goes up. In India the subsidy for fertilizers was Rs. 600 million in 1976–1977. It rose to Rs. 403 billion in 2007–2008, and reached Rs. 966 billion—or nearly a trillion—in 2008–2009.[16] These subsidies go to agribusiness, not farmers, who in turn fall deeper into debt traps as a result of these rising prices. Since synthetic fertilizers come from nonrenewable resources, they will eventually run out, though not before they have depleted the soil's renewable sources of fertility: its living organisms.

We are soil. We are earth. We are made of the same five elements—earth, water, fire, air, and space—that constitute the universe. What we do to soil, we do to ourselves; it is not an accident that "humus" and "humans" have the same etymological root.

This ecological truth is forgotten in the dominant knowledge paradigm, because industrial agriculture is based on eco-apartheid. It is based on the false idea that we are separate from and independent of the earth. It is based on a worldview that defines soil as dead matter. If soil is dead to begin with, human action cannot destroy its life; it can only "improve" the soil with chemical fertilizers. And if we are masters and conquerors of the soil, we determine the fate of the soil.

> It has been the assumption of the Green Revolution that nutrient loss and nutrient deficit can be made up by the use of non-renewable inputs of phosphorous, potash, and nitrates as chemical fertilizers. Under the industrial paradigm of agriculture, the nutrient cycle—in which nutrients are produced by soil through plants and returned to the soil as organic matter—has been replaced by linear, non-renewable flows of phosphorous and potash derived from geological deposits, and nitrogen derived from petroleum.[17]

But even Howard's early work showed that "the foundation of all good cultivation lies not so much in the plant as in the soil."[18] While at his experimental station, Howard showed that taking care of living soil that nourishes the plant can have more significant contributions to farming than simply breeding plants without improving the soil. Where breeding alone contributed to a 10 percent increase in yield, soil fertility improvement through organic matter and green manures contributed to a 200–300 percent increase.[19]

At our farm at Navdanya, we find the same trends. Our farm began on a piece of land left barren and sandy by a eucalyptus plantation imported from Australia to India, where the trees cannot participate in the Law of Return. Their leaves do not degrade, they take up too much water, and they release allopathic terpenes that prevent the growth of any other plants. The land had no soil organisms and no water-holding capacity. With love we grew diversity, and gave back as much organic matter to the soil as possible. Today, the soil is thriving with organisms, earthworm molds cover the farm, and we have been able to reduce water use by 70 percent because the soil can now hold water. The soil teems with life and gives us life.

Healthy soils produce healthy plants, and as Howard once stated, "the birthright of every crop is health."[20] This is especially true in times of climate change. Industrial agriculture is responsible for 40 percent of the greenhouse gases contributing to climate change, and heavily fertilized monocultures are more vulnerable to climate chaos.

During a 2009 countrywide drought in India, when I visited Navdanya farmers in different parts of the country, I found their crops had not suffered, because they were using locally adapted seeds, and their soils had water-holding capacity because of organic manuring. Farmers using Green Revolution, fertilizer-intensive varieties, or GMO Bt cotton, had a crop failure because neither the seed nor the soil was drought resilient.

Growing diversity and growing organic have become necessary for adapting our soils to climate change. Supporting healthy soils is the most effective way to get carbon dioxide out of the atmosphere. Soils with organic matter are more resilient to drought and climate extremes. Biodiversity-intensive systems—which are, in effect, photosynthesis-intensive systems—drive carbon dioxide out of the atmosphere and into plants and then into the soil. Soil, not oil, holds the future for humanity. Oil-based, fossil-fuel-intensive, chemical-intensive industrial agriculture unleashes processes that are killing the soil, and hence terminating our future.

History bears witness to the fact that the fate of societies and civilizations is intimately connected to how we treat the soil: do we relate to soil through the Law of Return or through the Law of Exploitation? The Law of Return, of giving back, has ensured that societies create and maintain fertile soil, and can be supported by living soil over thousands of years. The Law of Exploitation, of taking without giving back, has led to the collapse of civilizations.

Contemporary societies across the world stand on the verge of collapse as soils are eroded, degraded, poisoned, buried under concrete, and deprived of their life. But it can go differently.

Howard had warned us nearly a century ago that

> We must look at our present civilization as a whole and realize once and for all the great principle that the activities of *homo sapiens,* which have created the machine age in which we are now living, are based on a very insecure basis—the surplus food made available by the plunder of stores of soil fertility which are not ours but the property of generations to come … No one generation has the right to exhaust the soil from which humanity must draw its sustenance.[21]

Indian poet and philosopher Rabindranath Tagore invites us to return to the soil and to make peace with the earth: [22]

> *Let us all return to the soil*
> *That lays the corners of its garments*
> *And waits for us.*
> *Life rears itself from her breast,*
> *Flowers bloom from her smiles*
> *Her call is the sweetest music;*
> *Her lap stretches from one corner to the other,*
> *She controls the strings of life.*
> *Her warbling waters bring*
> *The murmur of life from all eternity.*

3

Bees and Butterflies Feed the World, Not Poisons and Pesticides

The destruction of a pest is the evasion of, rather than the solution [for], all agricultural problems.
—SIR ALBERT HOWARD[1]

Bees, butterflies, insects, and birds move pollen from flower to flower, fertilizing plants and allowing them to reproduce. Without pollinators, most plants would not reproduce, and without plant reproduction, our food supply would be threatened. The cycle of seed, whether it is for trees in the forests or crops that make up the food we eat, relies on cycles of pollination.

Ecologically biodiverse systems do not just protect bees and pollinators that feed us; they also control pests through a natural pest/predator balance. They support an abundance of natural enemies, which prevent the explosion of pest populations. Industrial monocultures, on the other hand, create a feast for pests, because there is no biodiversity to provide the ecological functions of pest control.

In the industrial paradigm of knowledge and agriculture, pest control is a matter of war. As a pest management textbook states, "The war against pests is a continuing one that man must fight to ensure his survival. Pests (in particular insects) are our major competitors on earth."[2]

More than fifty years ago, Rachel Carson wrote *Silent Spring*, an early warning for future generations. She questioned the changing world around her:

> There was a strange stillness. The birds, for example—where had they gone? The few birds seen anywhere were moribund; they trembled violently and could not fly.... On the farms the hens brooded, but no chicks hatched.... The apple trees were coming into bloom but no bees droned among the blossoms, so there was no pollination and there would be no fruit.... It was a spring without voices.[3]

Carson's now-iconic book explored the hazardous ecological consequences of chemicals and pesticides, warning that the deadly chemicals silencing the sounds of spring would not spare human beings either. Today her warning has become a widespread reality, and there are poisons everywhere in our food system.

Over the past four decades we have witnessed a drastic increase in the use of pesticides that have their origins in chemical warfare. Pesticides are not only devastating to the ecosystem and to friendly pollinators, but to our health. And because pesticide corporations are often also in the business of pharmaceuticals and seeds, these chemicals are unethically marketed as safe "medicines" for plants and as food providers for humans. In countries where farmers tend to be poor and illiterate, this pervasive and dangerous packaging of toxins has been difficult to subvert. Furthermore, given the large amounts of money to be made by agribusiness, the use of harmful pesticides remains unchallenged by government agencies that are actually supposed to protect people from harm.

But pesticides do not control pests; rather, they *create* them. Pests increase with the application of pesticides because beneficial species are killed and pests become resistant to chemicals. Promoters of agribusiness have argued that there has been a recent outbreak of pests that must be controlled. But in reality, both pesticides and GMOs—which were designed as supposed alternatives to pesticides—are threatening our natural systems of pest control: pollinators. Outbreaks of pests are symptoms of a system that is out of balance; instead of deepening the imbalance by introducing more deadly poisons to kill pests, we must restore the natural balance of pollinators and pests, and thus restore health and nutrition in our food and sustainable life in our ecosystems.

On December 25, 1925, I. G. Farben, a German chemical conglomerate, was constituted in a merger of existing chemical companies that included BASF, Bayer, and Hoechst. In the 1920s and 1930s, I. G. Farben screened Zyklon B for Hitler's extermination effort and used nerve gases on victims of the Holocaust in concentration camps. Others involved in the trials with nerve gases were DuPont, Shell, Union Carbide, Basel AG (Ciba, Geigy, and Sandoz), American Cyanamid, and Rhône-Poulenc—all companies that are today well known for the chemicals, pesticides, or oil they deal in. This is because following the war, companies specializing in the genocide of human beings turned their attention elsewhere.

In a chapter entitled "Elixirs of Death" in *Silent Spring*, Rachel Carson indicates how the end of World War II signaled the mass entry of pesticides into our crops and into our food. She writes, "In the course of developing agents of chemical warfare, some of the chemicals created in the lab were found to be lethal to insects—some of them became deadly nerve gases [and] others, of closely allied structure, became insecticides."[4]

Today there are up to 1,400 pesticides used globally in agriculture.[5] Pesticides fall into five categories: herbicides, used to destroy unwanted weeds and plants; insecticides, used to kill insects and other arthropods; rodenticides, to control mice and other rodents; fungicides, used to destroy fungi; and molluscicides, used against mollusks.[6]

Ideally, these pesticides should act only on the target organism.

However, only 1 percent of the pesticide sprayed acts on the target, and the rest spreads into the ecosystem, affecting all organisms. Pesticides are highly nonspecific and are toxic to many nontarget organisms, including humans. A 1990 report from the World Health Organization (WHO) states that "There is no segment of the general population that is sheltered from exposure to pesticides and potentially serious health effects, although a disproportionate burden is shouldered by the developing world and high-risk groups in each country."[7]

Apart from being sprayed, pesticides also coat most of the seeds that are purchased in markets today. Seed coating is a technique in which several materials, including fertilizers, nutritional elements, plant growth regulators, chemicals, and pesticides, are added to seeds through adhesive agents that are supposed to "enhance seed performance" and stop "seed diseases." But these diseases are a direct result of the pesticide-based monocultures in which seeds are planted. Pesticides create more pests, and seeds from pest-infested crops carry diseases. The pesticide industry then finds a new market: coating seeds with pesticides under the argument that this decreases crop losses. This is a self-perpetuating vicious cycle.[8] In India, all commercially sold seeds are coated with pesticides.[9] In the United States, 90 percent of all corn seeds are coated with Bayer's neonicotinoid pesticides, which are deeply implicated in bee deaths.[10]

The manufacture and use of pesticides is continuously increasing. New chemicals are introduced in the market regularly, and the system of registering and controlling pesticides by governments is greatly flawed and can be manipulated in accordance with corporate interests. The increase is especially seen in the Global South, where the use of pesticides is growing at the rate of 5–7 percent per year. Pesticides are now found in our rivers, groundwater, breast milk, soil, food, and air. Consumption of food is a key route of human exposure to pesticides and industrial pollutants. We are all exposed to pesticides and carry measurable amounts of these harmful chemicals in our bodies. The full effects of these pesticides that we ingest through our daily diets are not entirely known, but studies demonstrate that the most harmful effects are on children, who consume greater quantities of food per unit of body weight. For example, infants in India are exposed to relatively more arsenic than the general population because infants consume more rice, which has a higher arsenic concentration.[11] In addition to the poisons that pesticides create in our food, pesticides also pose serious health risks to those working with them, especially farmers, or those living in close proximity to the factories in which they are produced.

I. G. Farben and others specialized in the development of sarin and tabun, chemicals that fall under a category known as organophosphates (OPs),[12] which were used as nerve gases in the Nazi concentration camps. Today, most of the pesticides sold in the market are nerve poisons, which means that they act on the nervous system. This explains both their effectiveness and their toxic potential. These pesticides, even in minute quantities, can damage the nervous system and hence can cause neuropsychiatric disorders, either chronic or long-lasting in their course.[13] Exposure to OPs can cause acute illness such as nausea, vomiting, headache, abdominal pain, dizziness, skin diseases, eye diseases, stillbirths, and birth defects.[14] I. G. Farben was tried for its role in the Holocaust during the Nuremberg trials that followed World War II. Its role in spreading a more recent, pesticide-based genocide has, however, gone largely unchecked.

In December 1984, what is widely considered to be the world's worst industrial disaster[15] occurred at a pesticide plant owned by Union Carbide—now owned by Dow—in Bhopal, India. A gas leak known as the Bhopal gas tragedy killed three thousand people overnight and has killed more than thirty thousand since. Countless animals and other nonhuman creatures also died in the forty-minute-long leak: a stark reminder that pesticides brutally kill everything in their path. The gas from the pesticide plant polluted drinking water and soil, following which two hundred women had stillbirths and four hundred babies died only days after they were born. According to official figures, ten thousand people were made permanently disabled, thirty thousand partially disabled, and one hundred fifty thousand people suffer from a minor impairment.[16]

Despite fighting a case against Dow for three decades, victims of the Bhopal gas tragedy have received no justice. Instead, Dow has repeatedly brought lawsuits against activists for nonviolent demonstrations calling for justice. Meanwhile, Dow is spreading its chemicals across the world. The new Agent Orange herbicide-resistant GMO—named for the herbicide sprayed by the British and US military during the Vietnam War—is a product developed by Dow and has been found by the US Institute of Medicine to be responsible for, among other diseases, soft-tissue sarcoma, non-Hodgkin's lymphoma, chronic lymphocytic leukemia, Hodgkin's disease, and chloracne.[17]

Pesticides in agriculture and food are killing farmworkers, consumers, children, butterflies, and bees. The Navdanya report "Poisons in Our Food" shows that there is a clear link between disease epidemics like cancer and the use of pesticides in agriculture. In Punjab, the land of the so-called Green Revolution where large amounts of pesticides are used on a daily basis, the cancer rate is disproportionately high. A train dubbed the "cancer train" leaves Punjab every day, carrying in it victims of cancer for free treatment in Rajasthan.

The devastating effects of poison in the human diet are far-reaching. Nearly seven hundred thousand Indians die of cancer each year, while more than a million are diagnosed with some form of the disease.[18] Globally, 8.3 million people died of cancer in 2012,[19] and the World Health Organization reports that 222,000 people die every year worldwide because of pesticide poisoning.[20] In 1960 in the United States, one in twenty people had cancer. By 1995, the figure had jumped to one in eight, due to increased pesticide use.[21]

A Sri Lankan study found links between the increasing use of glyphosate (used under the Monsanto brand Roundup Ready) and kidney disease, which has affected four hundred thousand farmers and killed twenty thousand in the last twenty years.[22] In the United States, according to the Centers for Disease Control and Prevention, autism has increased by 35 percent in two years, from one in eighty-five children to one in sixty-eight children. The center suggests the causes are environmental, where the increasing use of glyphosate and GMOs are the most significant environmental changes.[23]

Growing data from across the world points to the fact that we can no longer ignore the hazardous and life-threatening costs of ever-increasing poisons in our food system. A corporate strategy to counter this data has been to try to silence, hound, and victimize scientists whose work shows that pesticides and GMOs cause harm to health. Examples include Arpad Pusztai of the United Kingdom, Gilles-Éric Séralini of France, Tyrone Hayes of the University of California, Berkeley, Vicki Vance of the University of South Carolina, and many others. I have called this "knowledge terrorism."

Given that only 1 percent of a pesticide application acts on the target "pest," the effect on friendly insects and pollinators is drastic. Pollinators contribute significantly to our food security and the agricultural economy.

Honeybees, for example, pollinate seventy-one of the one hundred most common crops that account for 90 percent of the world's food supply. Globally, the contribution of bees to crop production has been estimated at $200 billion.[24] One out of every four mouthfuls of food in the world is produced by the ecological contributions of pollinators.[25] Insect-pollinated crops in the United States are valued at $20 billion.[26] Yet bees and butterflies, which are essential food producers, are being killed by the arsenal of poisons that form the basis of industrial agriculture.

From 1985 to 1997 the number of honeybee colonies in US farmland dropped by approximately 57 percent. Pesticides were largely responsible for this change. The immune system of honeybees weakens on exposure to pesticides, and they become more vulnerable to natural enemies. Exposure to pesticides can also disrupt their reproduction and development. Pollinators are an essential natural service provided to farmers, and without their existence, our very food security is under threat.[27]

US scientist Paul DeBach writes:

> The philosophy of pest control by chemicals has been to achieve the highest kill possible, and percent mortality has been the main yardstick in the early screening of new chemicals in the lab. Such an objective, the highest kill possible, combined with ignorance of, or

disregard for, non-target insects and mites, is guaranteed to be the quickest road to upset resurgences and the development of resistance to pesticides.[28]

Many large war companies that became the agrochemical industry later became the seed industry through genetic engineering. Of these companies, US-based Monsanto has a monopoly, owning 23 percent of the global proprietary seed market.[29] In the United States, where GM crops are widespread, 80 percent of corn and 93 percent of soy grown is from Monsanto-patented GM seeds. Worldwide, 282 million acres of land are used for Monsanto crops (from 3 million in 1996).[30]

Genetic engineering was offered as an alternative to chemical pesticides. However, GM crops are part of the same logic of war against nature promoted by the Law of Domination and a militaristic paradigm. In the case of GMOs, the poison has been introduced as a toxin-producing gene within the plant, so in effect, the GMO becomes a pesticide-producing plant. Just as pesticides created pests instead of controlling them, GMOs as pesticide-producing plants also increase pests instead of controlling them. New pests emerge and old pests become resistant. The result is an increased use of chemical pesticides.

GMOs are failing to control pests and weeds. Instead, they have created superpests and superweeds. In twenty years of the commercialization of genetically engineered crops, only two traits have been commercialized on a significant scale: herbicide tolerance and insect resistance. Herbicide-tolerant crops, known under the Monsanto brand name Roundup Ready, were supposed to control weeds, and Bt crops were intended to control pests. In 2013, Food and Water Watch calculated that 27 percent of Monsanto's profits came from the sale of Roundup Ready herbicide.[31] But instead of controlling weeds and pests, these GM crops have led to the emergence of superweeds and superpests. In the United States, Roundup Ready crops have produced weeds resistant to Roundup. Approximately fifteen million acres are now overtaken by superweeds, and, in an attempt to kill these weeds, farmers have been paid $12 per acre by Monsanto to spray more lethal herbicides, such as

Agent Orange, which was used during the Vietnam War.

Herbicide-resistant plants such as Roundup Ready corn and soy have led to the increased use of glyphosate (present in herbicides), which kills all other plants, including milkweed: the only type of plant that monarch butterflies use for laying their eggs. Monarch butterflies are essential pollinators for crops, and some of the most beautiful butterflies in the world. As Roundup Ready crops have increased to 90 percent, milkweed has declined by 60 percent, and the number of monarch butterflies that migrate across the United States each year into Mexico has dropped from 1 billion in 1997 to an all-time low of 33.5 million.[32]

In India, Bt cotton sold under the trade name Bollgard was supposed to control the bollworm pest. Today the bollworm has become resistant to Bt cotton, and now Monsanto is selling Bollgard II, which carries two additional toxic genes within it. Field studies carried out by Navdanya and the Research Foundation for Science, Technology and Ecology in 2008 have shown that pesticide use in Vidarbha in Maharashtra has increased thirteenfold after the introduction of Bt cotton. A recent study also shows that there is a higher expenditure on chemical pesticides for Bt cotton than for other crop varieties.[33]

These statistics are not unique to India. A study by Charles Benbrook reports that herbicide-resistant crop technology has led to a 239 million kg increase in herbicide use in the United States between 1996 and 2011, while Bt crops have generally reduced insecticide applications by 56 million kg. Overall, this still means that pesticide use has increased by an estimated 183 million kg, or about 7 percent. Additionally, the reduction in insecticide use isn't true for all crops. While the introduction of Bt corn has had no impact on the use of chemicals, in Alabama, where Bt cotton is widely planted, the use of insecticides *doubled* between 1997 and 2008.[34]

Moreover, the same report also found that in 2008, GM crops required 26 percent more pounds of pesticides per acre than acres planted with conventional varieties, and projects that this trend will continue due to the spread of glyphosate-resistant weeds.[35] The rise of glyphosate-resistant weeds has made it necessary to combat these weeds by employing other, often more toxic, herbicides. This trend is confirmed by 2010 US Department of Agriculture pesticide data,[36] which shows that skyrocketing glyphosate use is accompanied by constant or increasing rates of use of other, more toxic, herbicides.

In China, since the introduction of Bt cotton in 1997, populations of mirid bugs, which previously posed only a minor problem to farmers, have increased twelvefold. A 2008 study in the *International Journal of Biotechnology* found that any financial benefits of planting Bt cotton were eroded by the increasing use of pesticides needed to combat non-target pests.[37]

In Argentina, after the introduction of Roundup Ready soy in 1999, the use of herbicides more than tripled by 2006. Roundup Ready soy growers use more than twice as much herbicide as conventional soy growers; and in 2007, a glyphosate-resistant version of Johnsongrass (considered one of the worst and most difficult weeds in the world) was reported on more than 120,000 hectares of prime agricultural land—a consequence of the increase in glyphosate use. It is estimated that an additional twenty-five liters of herbicides will be needed annually per farmer to control the resistant weeds.[38] Across what is known as the "GM belt" in Argentina, citizens are complaining about growing health risks—including cancer and birth defects—linked to the aggressive spraying of agrochemicals.[39]

In Brazil, which has been the world's largest consumer of pesticides since 2008, GM crops make up 45 percent of all row crops planted in the country. This percentage is only expected to rise.[40]

Benbrook's study of the use of pesticides in the United States concludes:

> Contrary to often-repeated claims that today's genetically-engineered crops have, and are reducing pesticide use, the spread of glyphosate-resistant weeds in herbicide-resistant weed management systems has brought about substantial increases in the number and volume of herbicides applied.... The magnitude of increases in herbicide use on

herbicide-resistant hectares has dwarfed the reduction in insecticide use on *Bt* crops over the past 16 years, and will continue to do so for the foreseeable future.[41]

Despite claims that GMOs will lower the levels of chemicals used, this has not been the case. This is of great concern both because of the negative impacts of these chemicals on ecosystems and humans, and because there is the danger that increased chemical use will cause pests and weeds to develop resistance, requiring even more chemicals in order to manage them.

This is not food production. This is war.

––––––––––

The CEO of agrochemical company Syngenta, Mike Mack, defended the use of GMOs at the World Economic Forum, stating, "There is very little about farming that's natural…. Farming's been around for 10,000 years, and a lot of [it] has been [spent] trying to keep the pests, however you do that, off the farm."[42]

But the war against pests is neither necessary nor effective. Pests are controlled when there is an ecological balance among diverse components in a farming system, and biodiversity is our best friend in dealing with pest problems. This works on two levels.

First, pests do not emerge in agricultural systems based on diversity, because in an agroecological farming system, no one insect, or weed, is a "pest." Ecological balance through biodiversity is the best pest control mechanism, and friendly insects such as ladybugs, beetles, soldier beetles, spiders, wasps, and the praying mantis all contribute to this process.

Biodiversity allows for systems of integrated pest control like the push-pull system, where one plant's role is to attract pests and another's is to repel them. This technique is used by thousands of farmers across eastern Africa who intercrop silverleaf desmodium (a fodder legume) with maize, napier, and Sudan grass. Aromas produced by the desmodium repel (push) pests like the maize stemborer, while scents produced by the grasses attract (pull) the stemborer and encourage them to lay their eggs in the grass instead of the maize. In turn, the napier grass produces a gummy substance that traps the stemborer larvae, so that once they hatch, only a few survive into adulthood, thus reducing their numbers.[43]

Countries across the world are adopting systems of integrated pest control based on biodiversity. In Indonesia, the Food and Agriculture Organization (FAO) worked together with the government to establish farmers' field schools to teach integrated pest management. This is widely considered to be one of the most successful examples of reducing dependence on pesticides through biodiversity.[44] In India, the state government of Andhra Pradesh has made a commitment to promote pesticide-free farming, and farmers within the state have both increased production and reduced costs.[45]

The second benefit of biodiversity is that if there is a pest outbreak, biodiversity offers ecological alternatives in the form of botanical pest control agents, such as neem. Neem (*Azadirachta indica*) is a tree indigenous to India that has spread worldwide because of its beneficial uses. In 1985 at the time of the Bhopal gas tragedy, I started a campaign with the slogan "No more Bhopals, plant a neem." Ten years later, I found that the use of neem had been patented by the US Department of Agriculture and W. R. Grace (a chemical company that was implicated in polluting groundwater outside Boston, which led to a cancer epidemic; the book and film *A Civil Action* were based on the case). With Magda Aelvoet from the Greens of the European Parliament, and Linda Bullard, the president of the International Federation of Organic Agriculture Movements, I filed a case challenging the biopiracy of neem. It took us eleven years, but we overturned the patent, and the use of neem as a natural form of pest control remains with nature and with farmers. In a biodiverse system, several plants that offer safe and effective pest control are allowed to flourish. Some of these plants are neem, dhaikan (*Melia azedarach*), nurgundi (*Vitex negundo*), sharifa (*Annona squamosa*), pongam or karanj (*Pongamia pinnata*), garlic (*Allium sativum*), and tobacco (*Nicotiana tabacum*).

People across the globe are fighting back against the use of pesticides and poisons in our food system. US beekeepers have sued chemical company Bayer after they lost thousands of bee colonies due to the pesticide treatment of canola seeds. In 1999, France banned Gaucho, a broad-spectrum insecticide, due to its toxicity to bees and other forms of life, including humans.[46]

On April 29, 2013, the European Union banned the use of neo-nicotinoids to protect bees. These neonicotinoids are sold under brand names that come straight from war artillery: Helix, Cruiser, Flagship, and Honcho. In Europe, neonicotinoids account for 16 percent of the €8 billion pesticide market, and 77 percent of the €535 million seed treatment market.[47] Tonio Borg, the European Commissioner for Health at the time, said they planned to implement the landmark ban starting December 2013. He stated, "I pledge to do my utmost to ensure that our bees, which are so vital to our ecosystem and contribute over 22 billion annually to European agriculture, are protected."[48] However, Bayer blocked this decision from going through and instead sued the European Commission in 2013 for attempting to restrict the use of pesticides.

On May 6, 2014, the Chinese government announced that GMO grain, food, and oil would no longer be supplied to its military personnel. The Hubei Province Xiangyang City Grain Bureau's website reads that "the safety concerns about GMO grain and oil products in China at present [have] not yet been determined [and] in order to overall assure the health of military members residing in our city" GMO food will be banned.[49] Even more significantly, in April 2014 Russia banned the import of any GMO products, with its prime minister Dmitry Medvedev commenting, "If the Americans like to eat GMO products, let them eat it then. We don't need to do that; we have enough space and opportunities to produce organic food."[50]

Both the organic movement—toward chemical-free, pesticide-free, GMO-free farming—as well as the environmental movement—against climate change—are trying to create a poison-free world. The imperative to spread poisons is not an ecological imperative for how nature works, nor is it a socioeconomic imperative for creating thriving economies. Rather, it is only an imperative for corporate profits, which have their roots in poisons from war. These corporations have subsequently become addicted both to the profits as well as a militarized mindset and paradigm of knowledge that make poisons appear essential for pest control, and by extension, for feeding the world.

But as we have seen, there are poison-free ways of farming that are not only possible but successful. Breaking out of the poison cycle is crucial to protecting both our health and our biodiversity, which are under threat from pesticides and pesticide-producing plants. Biodiversity and ecological processes are the most sophisticated and proven approach to controlling pests. It is time to make a paradigm shift from the militarized mind, which sees all species as enemies to be exterminated, to a worldview that sees humans as part of an Earth Family and that recognizes pollinators and friendly insects as our coproducers in the food web.

WAR ARSENAL

Achieve, Action, Aim, Ally, Ambush, Ammo, Apocalypse, Arsenal, Assert, Authority First, Avenge, Barrage, Bicep II, Boundary, Bravo, Brawl, Brigade, Broadstrike, Bullet, Cadet, Cadre, Capture, Champion, Charger, Clincher, Cobra, Command, Contain, Cyclone, Disrupt, Domain, Dual Magnum, Eminent, Enforcer, Extreme, Falcon, Firestorm, Firstshot, Force, Frontier, Fury, Fusilade, Gunslinger, Havoc, Hi-Yield Killzall, Honcho, Honor Guard, Ignite, Impact, Infantry 4l, Javelin, Jury, Lasso, Lightning, Machete, Pentagon, Pounce, Prowl, Quick Kill, Rampage, Revenge, Revolver, Roundup, Saber, Savage, Scepter, Shotgun, Sledgehammer, Squadron, Subdue, Total Kill, Trigger, Vanquish

Sources: Vandana Shiva, *Staying Alive* (New Delhi: Kali Unlimited, 2010); Joni Seager, *Carson's Silent Spring* (New York: Bloomsbury, 2014).

4

Biodiversity Feeds the World, Not Toxic Monocultures

More than seven thousand species have fed humanity throughout history: a remarkable indication of the biodiversity on our planet. In a biodiverse farming system, thousands of insects pollinate our crops and give us food. Friendly insects control pests by maintaining a natural pest-predator balance. Millions of soil organisms work to create life and fertility in the soil. Fertile and healthy soils give us abundant and healthy food. On a biodiverse farm, ecosystem, or planet, the food web is the web of life.

But today, just thirty crops provide 90 percent of the calories in the human diet, and only three species—rice, wheat, and maize—account for more than 50 percent of our calorie intake. According to the State of the World's Plant Genetic Resources for Food and Agriculture, of the 7,098 apple varieties documented in the United States in the beginning of the twentieth century, 96 percent have been lost. Additionally, 95 percent of the cabbage, 91 percent of the field maize, 94 percent of the pea, and 81 percent of the tomato varieties have also been lost. In Mexico, of all the varieties of corn reported in 1930, only 20 percent exist today.[1]

The loss of biodiversity in our food and on our land is because industrial agriculture systems promote monocultures. Monocultures are based on the cultivation of only one variety of one crop, which is bred to respond to externally applied chemicals or toxins.

The rapid erosion of biodiversity has taken place under a food system that sees farms as factories for commodities rather than webs of food production and life. These factories run on chemicals that were once designed for warfare, and are destroying the diverse species that have flourished on our planet for millennia. Biodiversity increases the stability of ecosystems and their ecological functions, whereas a reduction in the number of genes, species, and groups of organisms reduces the efficiency and resilience of whole communities.[2]

Three forces have driven the disappearance of biodiversity across the world, and all three are connected to the corporate control over seed. The first is the entry of big business into the seed market, which has displaced local diverse varieties evolved by farmers with uniform, commercial hybrids and GMOs engineered and sold by corporations. Whereas once we had differently shaped, nutritious, and seasonal fruits, today we have uniform varieties available all year round. The second factor is globalization-driven long-distance trade. Diversity goes hand in hand with local, decentralized food systems, but in a global food system, freshness and softness are replaced by hardness, so that fruits can travel. We are breeding rocks, not fruit. The third factor is industrial processing, which leads to companies like McDonald's and PepsiCo replacing nutritious, local dishes with junk-food commodities. This then influences what crops are grown. For example, juicy, tasty tomatoes disappear to make way for hard, tasteless ones, because tomato ketchup requires the latter. Today, every cuisine deserves to be recognized as cultural heritage before it is wiped out.

Biodiversity, food diversity, and cultural diversity go hand in hand. Tribals in the heartland of India evolved two hundred thousand rice varieties from one wild grass: the *Oryza sativa*. Rice is their life, rice is their food, and rice is their culture. I have joined them at Akti, the festival that marks the beginning of the agricultural cycle where they bring their diverse rice varieties, offer them to the village deity, share them with each other, and then sow the rice in their fields. Or take Mexico, where thousands of years ago, peasants domesticated a wild plant called *teosinte* and transformed and evolved it into the diversity of thousands of corn varieties. Mexicans are the people of corn: corn is their identity, their food, and their culture.

The corporate control of seed that has eroded biodiversity is a result of a paradigm of production based on uniformity and monocultures: what I have called Monocultures of the Mind. A Monoculture of the Mind imposes one way of knowing—reductionist and mechanistic—on a world with a diversity and plurality of knowledge systems. These knowledge systems include the knowledge and expertise that come from practice, experience, and working with nature as a partner: the knowledge of women and workers, and of farmers and peasants. These knowledge systems are multiple and diverse. But as ecological biodiversity is replaced by monocultures of food and crops that can be commodified and patented for profits, and as the rich diversity of food cultures is being replaced by monocultures of junk food, the human mind is also being reduced to a monoculture. Monocultures of the Mind, rooted in a reductionist, mechanistic paradigm, create a blindness to the diversity of the world. Based on mechanistic thought, these monocultures are blind to the evolutionary potential and intelligence of cells, organisms, ecosystems, and communities. They are blind to the ecological functions arising from the relationships and cooperation between diverse living components of an agroecosystem. And in a vicious cycle of uniformity, these Monocultures of the Mind once again perpetuate monocultures on the land.

A mechanistic paradigm of industrial agriculture converts diversity to monocultures by focusing on external inputs of chemicals as well as on uniform monoculture commodities as outputs. We have been falsely led to believe that chemical-intensive monocultures produce more food and are therefore the answer to hunger and food insecurity. The same mechanized thinking promotes the idea that by intensifying monocultures through inputs of toxic chemicals, fossil fuels, and capital, biodiversity will be conserved because less land will be used. This is false.

Chemical-intensive monocultures produce less food per acre than biodiverse, ecological farms when all outputs are taken into account. Monocultures displace diversity on a farm, and according to the UN International Technical Conference for Plant Genetic Resources in Leipzig, Germany, in 1995, 75 percent of all agro-biodiversity has been displaced because of industrial monocultures in agriculture. We can safely assume that this percentage has only grown.

Industrial agriculture is based on external inputs of chemical pesticides as well as GMO crops with pesticides built into them, which kill beneficial species and undermine food production. These chemicals come from war. And through industrial agriculture, they continue the war. The false productivity of industrial agriculture has been manipulated at every level by ignoring the contributions of the biodiversity of plants, soil organisms, and pollinators to agriculture and food production. Through a mechanistic, reductionist framework, a myth has been created that without chemical monocultures we will have no food, and that biodiverse, organic farming is more expensive and a luxury for the wealthy.

We must dismantle these myths. Under the industrial paradigm, toxic chemicals kill the biodiversity of bees, butterflies, and friendly insects. Chemical fertilizers kill soil organisms, destroying the soil and soil fertility. Nitrogen fertilizers create dead zones and kill the biodiversity of aquatic and marine life. Furthermore, because they rely heavily on inputs of deadly chemicals, the cost to both the farmer and the consumer is greater in monoculture farming; the only profits being made are by large agribusinesses. Monocultures of the Mind focus on only one economy: the global market controlled by global corporations.

They remain blind to the economies of nature and society, to nature's economy, and to people's sustenance economy. We need to put an end to monocultures, both on land and in the human mind, and we need to urgently assess the true costs of industrial agriculture and the true benefits of biodiverse, ecological farming.

Biodiverse systems of mixed cropping are based on a symbiotic relationship between soil, water, farm animals, and plants. Ecological agriculture links these elements together in sustainable ways, where each is dependent on the other, and the relationship between them is thus strengthened. Green Revolution agriculture, or industrial agriculture, replaces this integration with the introduction of external inputs, such as seeds that are bred for responding to chemicals, or with the chemicals themselves.[3] Not only does the seed/chemical package break ecological farming interlinkages, but it also sets up its own toxic interactions with soil and with water systems. But these new interactions are not taken into account when measuring either the cost or the yields of industrial farming.

Diversity has been destroyed in agriculture under the false assumption that it is associated with low productivity. As a result, farmers' diverse, native varieties have been replaced by new crops that are misleadingly called high yielding varieties, or HYVs. HYVs are part of the first myth that has been used to push industrial, monoculture farm systems: that chemical farming produces more food. What multinational companies conveniently forget to tell us is that HYVs are not *intrinsically* high yielding. Rather, they respond well to chemicals (most likely produced by the same seed companies promoting HYVs). In fact, a more appropriate label for them would be "high *response* varieties."

Such varieties have been bred to yield enhanced grain production only with high levels of chemical inputs. If we look at a farming system as an ecosystem that feeds not only humans, but all living beings on the farm, HYVs exhibit very low total system productivity. In countries like India, for example, the quantity of straw that is obtained from grain is important as fodder for livestock. HYVs fail to produce a sufficient quantity or quality of straw, so that corporations can increase the marketable output of grain. But animals on the farm still have to eat, and so they are fed the very grain that was intended for humans. This grain is insufficient in terms of both nutrition and quantity for animals. Neither soil nor animals nor humans benefit from HYVs, and the increase in the marketable output of grain has been achieved at the cost of a decreased biomass for animals and soils, and decreased ecosystem productivity due to an overuse of resources.

Farmers' indigenous varieties outperform HYVs if we take into account the total biomass in a farming system. In fact, many native varieties have higher yields both in terms of grain output as well as in terms of total biomass output (grain plus straw) than the HYVs that have been introduced in their place. A study that compares traditional polycultures with industrial monocultures shows that a polyculture system can produce 100 units of food from 5 units of inputs, whereas an industrial system requires 300 units of input to produce the same 100 units of food. The 295 units of wasted inputs could have provided 5,900 units of additional food on a biodiverse farm. Thus, the industrial system leads to a decline of 5,900 units of food. This is a recipe for starving people, not for feeding them.[4]

The measurement of yield and productivity in the Green Revolution paradigm is divorced from an understanding of how the processes of increasing a single function of a single species affect the processes that sustain the conditions for agricultural production. This takes place by reducing the number of species and the functional diversity of farming systems, as well as by replacing internal inputs provided by biodiversity with hazardous agrochemicals. While these reductionist categories of yield and productivity allow for a higher measure of harvestable yields of single commodities, they exclude the measurement of the ecological destruction that affects future yields and the destruction of diverse outputs from biodiversity-rich systems.

Productivity in traditional farming practices has always been high, because it requires very few external inputs. So while the Green Revolution has been portrayed as having increased productivity in the absolute sense, when resource utilization is taken into account, it has lower productivity both in the sense of total biomass production as well as in the use of external inputs. Industrial chemical agriculture uses 10 kcal in inputs to produce 1 kcal of food. It also uses ten times more water and a lot more land than ecological agriculture to produce the same amount of food. The extra resources used by monocultures could have gone to feed people. Resources wasted amount to the creation of hunger. By being resource wasteful through one-dimensional monocultures maintained through intensive external inputs, new biotechnologies create food insecurity and starvation.

A common argument used in promoting genetic engineering in agriculture is that only industrial agriculture and industrial breeding can keep up with the increasing food needs of a growing population. Increased mouths to feed require a more efficient use of resources. But a study in the *Scientific American* shows that industrial agriculture has led to a sixtyfold *decrease* in food-producing capacity and is not an efficient strategy for using limited land, water, and biodiversity to feed the world.[5]

Furthermore, since food security is based on food entitlements—or access to food—and entitlements in peasant societies are based on livelihoods and work, an increase in food availability should not be based on the destruction of livelihoods. From the frame of reference of both food productivity and food entitlements, industrial agriculture is deficient as compared to a diversity-based internal input system in meeting the food needs of a growing population. Based on the Law of Return, biodiverse, ecological agriculture helps farmers on two levels. First, by working with ecological processes rather than against them, it frees farmers from costly purchased inputs that are trapping them in debt. Second, the Law of Return in society enables farmers and eaters to create relationships of fair trade, where farmers get a just price for their work creating good food and health and for being the stewards of our planet.

Agribusiness, governed by the Law of Exploitation and the Law of Domination, tells us that monocultures are the most cost-effective way of producing food, through both chemical farming and genetic engineering. But monoculture farming is a losing economy. As early as 1978, Professor William Lockeretz compared the economic performance of fourteen organic crop and livestock farms in the Midwestern United States with that of fourteen conventional, or monoculture, farms. The study farms were paired on the basis of physical characteristics and types of farm enterprises. The market value of crops produced per unit area was 11 percent less on the organic farms. But since the cost of production was also less, because organic farming relies less on external inputs such as chemicals and fertilizers, the net income per unit area was nearly equal for both systems. Monoculture farming is not more profitable than organic farming.

Because organic farmers grow a greater diversity of crops, the entire production on a farm is not vulnerable to the same pests or seasonal weather events. Additionally, organically farmed soils absorb more of the available rainfall, providing protection from drought.[6] If there is a total crop failure, organic farmers suffer fewer economic losses, because they have invested less in purchased inputs. The diversity of crops on organic farms also has other economic benefits. Diversity provides some protection from adverse price changes in a single commodity and provides a better seasonal distribution of inputs.

Organic farmers need to borrow less money than conventional farmers for two reasons. First, organic farmers buy fewer inputs, such as fertilizer and pesticides. Second, costs and income are more evenly distributed throughout the year on diversified, organic farms, because different crops are ready for harvesting at different points in the year. In India, the epidemic of farmers' suicides is concentrated in regions where chemical intensification has increased the costs of production and cash crop monocultures are facing a decline in prices and incomes due to globalization. High costs of production are the most significant reason for rural indebtedness, in an equation where monocultures = chemicals = debt = suicides.

When we consider all the data, the argument that there is a larger amount of cheaper food available through monocultures is illusionary on four counts. First, monocultures focus on the partial aspects of single crops rather than total system yields of multiple crops and integrated systems. Second, industrial breeding focuses on yields of one or two global commodities, not on the diverse crops that people actually eat. Here, the focus is on quantity per acre rather than nutrition per acre, when in fact, nutrition per acre has been reduced as a result of industrial agriculture. Third, industrial breeding, including genetic engineering, uses natural resources intensively and wastefully. If productivity is defined on the basis of resource use, industrial agriculture has very low productivity and undermines food security by using up resources that in a sustainable system of production could have been directly used to produce more food. Fourth, and crucially, chemical intensification and genetic engineering in monocultures produces *less* food than ecological alternatives that are based on biodiversity intensification.

———————

According to the dominant paradigm of food production, diversity hinders productivity. This creates an imperative for uniformity and monocultures, and has generated a paradoxical situation in which modern plant "improvement" has been based on the destruction of the biodiversity it then uses as a raw material. The irony of plant and animal breeding is that it destroys the very building blocks on which the technology depends. Forestry development schemes introduce monocultures of industrial species such as eucalyptus, and push into extinction the diversity of local species that once fulfilled local needs. Agricultural modernization schemes introduce new and uniform crops into farmers' fields and destroy the diversity of local varieties. Modernization of animal husbandry destroys diverse breeds and introduces factory farming.

This strategy of basing productivity increase on the destruction of diversity is dangerous and unnecessary. Monocultures are ecologically and socially nonsustainable because they destroy both nature's economy and people's economy. In agriculture, forestry, fisheries, and animal husbandry, production is being incessantly pushed in the direction of diversity destruction. Production based on uniformity thus becomes the primary threat to biodiversity conservation and to ecological and socioeconomic sustainability.

Diversity must first be made the logic of production before it can be conserved. If production continues to be based on the logic of uniformity and homogenization, uniformity will continue to displace diversity. "Improvement" from the corporate viewpoint, or from the viewpoint of Western agricultural or forestry research, is often a loss for the Global South, and especially for the poor in the Global South. Plant improvement in agriculture has been based on the enhancement of the yield of desired products at the expense of unwanted plant parts. The "desired" product is, however, not the same for agribusiness and for peasants, and which parts of a farming system will be treated as "unwanted" depends on what class, caste, or gender one belongs to. What is unwanted for agribusiness may be wanted by the poor, and by squeezing out those aspects of biodiversity, "agricultural development" fosters poverty and ecological decline. There is therefore no truth in the myth that production runs counter to diversity. Uniformity as a pattern of production becomes inevitable only in a context of control and profitability.

Productivity and sustainability are much higher in mixed systems of farming and forestry that produce diverse outputs. The productivity of monocultures is low in the context of diverse outputs and needs. It is high only in the restricted context of the output of "a part of a part" of the forest and farm biomass. "High yielding" Green Revolution cropping patterns pick one crop among hundreds—for example, wheat—for yields from only one part of the wheat plant: grain. These high partial yields do not translate into high total yields. Productivity is therefore different depending on whether it is measured in a framework of diversity or in a framework of uniformity, and whether it is understood through the Law of Return or the Law of Domination.

In this way, the economic calculations of agricultural productivity in the dominant paradigm distort real measures of productivity. They leave out the benefits of internal inputs derived from biodiversity and fail to account for the additional financial and ecological costs generated by the purchase of external, chemical inputs as substitutes for internal, natural inputs in monoculture systems.

The higher productivity of diversity-based systems indicates that there is an alternative to genetic engineering and industrial agriculture: an alternative that is more ecological and more equitable. This alternative is based on biodiversity intensification instead of chemical intensification. But even though diversity produces more than monocultures do, monocultures are profitable to industry, both for markets and for political control. The shift from high yielding diversity to low yielding monocultures is made possible because of a market logic that takes resources from the poor and gives them to the rich, only to then be destroyed. Meanwhile, higher commodity production brings benefits only to those with economic power, and ironically, it is the hunger of the poor that is used to justify the agricultural strategies that deepen their hunger.

While collecting seeds in a tribal region of Tamil Nadu in southern India, I met a farmer growing nine crops together. He explained how the diversity of crops on the land is connected from the macro to the micro: from the planetary balance of the solar system to the ecological balance of the Earth to the nutritional balance in our bodies. *Navdanya* means "nine seeds," or "nine crops," and as a testament to this diversity, I named our seed saving movement Navdanya.

The idea that "diversity is prosperity" is as old as it is true, and its practice can be seen across the living planet. Local mountain farmers in the Garhwal Himalayas have developed complementary and synergistic associations among different species to foster agrobiodiversity-centered agricultural practices. Of these, the *baranaaja* culture is a prime example and a testimony to prosperity in diversity. *Baranaaja* consists of twelve food grains intercropped with finger millet, which is used as the base crop. Amaranth, buckwheat, kidney beans, horse gram, black soybean, black gram, green gram, cowpea, rice bean, adzuki bean, sorghum, and cleome are the crops generally intermixed with finger millet. *Baranaaja* helps provide the maximum number of food items while ensuring a balanced diet from a minimum area of land. *Baranaaja* crops occupy the least fertile areas of cropland where other moisture-loving or water-guzzling crops would fail to grow. Such carefully crafted biodiversity management enhances the sustainability of the agroecosystem and raises the food security level of the entire farming community.

Several oceans away from the Himalayan mountain range, farmers of Mesoamerica have used a mixed-cropping system known as *milpa* for centuries. Based on the ancient agricultural methods of the Maya, Zapotec, and other Mesoamerican peoples, *milpa* agriculture produces maize (corn), beans, and squash, along with other crops suitable to local conditions. The system is entirely self-sustaining in regard to levels of consumption, and includes avocados, melons, tomatoes, chiles, sweet potatoes, jicama, amaranth, and mucuna. Journalist and author Charles C. Mann describes *milpa* as "nutritionally and environmentally complementary." He writes:

> Maize lacks the amino acids lysine and tryptophan, which the body needs to make proteins and niacin.... Beans have both lysine and tryptophan.... Squashes, for their part, provide an array of vitamins; avocados, fats. The milpa, in the estimation of H. Garrison Wilkes, a maize researcher at the University of Massachusetts in Boston, "is one of the most successful human inventions ever created."[7]

In San Felipe del Agua, *milpa* is more than the fields and crops: it is a network of families, commerce, and practices, much of which is very old. The *milpa* of San Felipe comprises traditional knowledge, handmade tools, the zebu-crossed criollo cattle used for plowing, burros, dogs, backyard tortilla factories, kitchen tables, meals, and hard work—it is a way of life centered around the maize, and a testament to not only biodiversity, but cultural diversity.

Variations of this organic practice (organic in terms of crops but also in terms of being rooted within a community) can be found across cultures. Among some Native American tribes, the *milpa* system takes the name "three sisters," bringing together corn, beans, and squash. By the time European settlers arrived in America in the early 1600s, the Iroquois had been growing the three sisters for more than three centuries. The vegetable trio sustained the Native Americans both physically and spiritually; in legend, the plants were a gift from the gods, always to be grown together, eaten together, and celebrated together.[8]

Both aspects of the food crisis—the agrarian crisis on the one hand and the malnutrition crisis on the other—are related to the fact that food production has become chemical-intensive and focused on "yield per acre." However, yield per acre ignores the loss of nutrition that is leading to the malnutrition crisis. So while the Green Revolution led to an increase of rice and wheat with chemical-intensive, capital-intensive, and water-intensive inputs, it simultaneously displaced pulses, oilseeds, millets, greens, vegetables, and fruits from the fields and from people's diets. Yield per acre is a measure of nothing but profits for agribusiness. Under the paradigm of agroecology, what we can measure instead is *nutrition* per acre.

Navdanya's report "Health Per Acre" shows that a shift to biodiverse organic farming and ecological intensification increases the output of nutrition while reducing input costs. For the study, we conducted field experiments in organic farms in which farmers grew twelve crops (*baranaaja*), nine crops (*navdanya*), and seven crops (*saptarshi*). In an acre of farmland, organic *baranaaja* produced 73.5 percent more protein, 3,200 percent more vitamins, 67 percent more minerals, and 186 percent more iron than conventional monoculture cropping did. Organic *navdanya* produced 355 percent more protein, 5,174 percent more vitamins, 57 percent more minerals, and 160 percent more iron than conventional monoculture cropping did, per acre of farmland. And finally, organic *saptarshi* produced 66 percent more protein, 54 percent more minerals, and 153 percent more iron than conventional monoculture cropping.[9] When agricultural output is measured in terms of "health per acre" and "nutrition per acre" instead of "yield per acre," biodiverse, ecological systems clearly have a much higher output.

Given the rapid changes and crises within our food system, there is an urgent need to monitor the ecological costs of the globalization of agriculture using a biodiversity-based productivity framework to reflect the health of nature's economy and people's economy. We at Navdanya have developed such a framework over the past three decades. This framework:

- provides documentation of the biodiversity status of a farm, including crop, tree, and animal biodiversity
- indicates the contribution of biodiversity to provisioning of internal inputs and to the building and maintenance of nature's economy through the conservation of soil, water, and biodiversity
- indicates the contribution of biodiversity to the self-provisioning of food needs by agricultural families and communities, and to the building and maintenance of people's economy
- reflects the market economy of the farm in terms of incomes from the sale of agricultural produce, as well as the additional costs for external inputs and retail food when biodiversity is lost

The paradigm shift we propose is a shift from monocultures to diversity; from chemical-intensive agriculture to ecologically intensive agriculture; from external inputs to internal inputs; from capital-intensive production to low- or zero-cost production; from yield per acre to health and nutrition per acre; and from food as a commodity to food as nourishment and nutrition. This shift addresses the multiple crises related to food systems: falling incomes for farmers, rising costs for consumers, and the increasing levels of pollution in our food.

Biodiverse organic farming leads to increased farm productivity and farm incomes, a lowering of costs to consumers through fair trade, and safe and healthy food for people and animals through pesticide-free and chemical-free production and processing. It shows how we can protect the environment while also protecting our farmers and our health. By maximizing health per acre and nurturing biodiversity, we can ensure that every human being has access to healthy, nutritious, safe, and good food.

5

Small-Scale Farmers Feed the World, Not Large-Scale Industrial Farms

In an age of obsession with gigantism, we live under the illusion that "big is best," that big produces more, that big is more powerful. When it comes to food, this translates into the idea that we need big farms and big corporations to feed the world. Today, just five corporations control the majority of seed, water, and land in the world, and they are growing.

But the reality is that "small is big"—ecologically, culturally, and economically.

The future of food security lies in protecting and promoting small-scale farmers. At the ecological level, in a small seed lies the potential for the largest tree. In each seed is the potential for multiplication into thousands of seeds. And in each of the thousands of those seeds are thousands and millions more. This is abundance from the small, not the large. That is why in India, while sowing seeds farmers pray, "May this seed be inexhaustible." In large-scale industrial farms, where seed is patented or biologically terminated by giant corporations, a seed cannot multiply or be reproduced. It produces zero seeds. The motto here seems to be "May this seed get exhausted so our profits are inexhaustible."

Despite threats from large companies, local farming communities still produce 70 percent of the world's food. These farming systems that have been around for centuries are governed by small-scale farmers and are steeped in diversity. On the one hand, they reflect diverse agroclimatic features, and on the other hand, they have developed within diverse food cultures. As we have seen, the diversity of agricultural systems and the cultural diversity of food systems have coevolved in a mutual interplay of nature and culture. Biodiversity and cultural diversity go hand in hand, and small is big culturally, too.

Economically speaking, it is often falsely assumed that small farms and small-scale farmers have low rates of production. But as we have seen, small, biodiverse farms are more ecologically efficient than large industrial monocultures. When one recognizes that small farms across the world produce greater and more diverse outputs of nutritious crops, it becomes clear that industrial breeding has actually *reduced* food security. Industrial farming has created hunger and poverty; yet large industrial farms are justified as necessary in order to produce more food.

The globalization of agriculture has led to the rapid destruction of diverse farming systems and the displacement of small-scale farmers worldwide. This in turn has led to a destruction of the environment and rural livelihoods, and especially farmers' livelihoods. Our nutritional, environmental, and cultural well-being is under threat. And in order to secure a future for ourselves and for all life on the planet, we must return to the kernel of truth we began with: small is big, and small is beautiful.

According to the dominant paradigm of industrial agriculture, intensifying chemical inputs and energy use is necessary for feeding a growing population because intensification of inputs and large farms lead to higher productivity and hence more food. This is not true. Productivity is the measure of output per unit of input. In terms of resources and energy, the higher the input, the lower the productivity. Since industrial agriculture is resource and energy intensive, it has led to a productivity decline in terms of ecological efficiency and resource-use efficiency.

In an ecological and small farming system, outputs include the rejuvenation of ecological processes, the diverse outputs of crops, livestock, and trees, and the livelihoods created through cocreation and coproduction. In a large-scale industrial farming system, output is reduced to a single commodity (the part of a part of a plant) and input is reduced to labor. The intensification of chemicals and fossil fuels is primarily aimed at substituting the labor of small-scale farmers and concentrating ownership of land in large farms owned by corporations. When labor is artificially selected as the only input that "counts," and productivity with respect to labor is seen as the only "real" productivity, an illusion is created. This illusion fosters a false sense of higher overall productivity and greater availability of food. In reality, more resources are being wasted, more livelihoods are being destroyed, and more hunger is being created.

When we use the term "livelihood," we are talking about self-organized work in living economies, based on cocreation and coproduction. A livelihood is not a "job." The word "job" was first used during the rise of the Industrial Revolution to describe piecework: a type of work that was measured by the number of items—or "pieces"—produced, such as garments or tools. The etymology is significant when we think of how the word "job" is used today. A "job" is based on the reduction of a creative, autonomous human being to "labor," and the further reduction of labor to a commodity. Peasants and small-scale farmers do not have jobs; they have livelihoods. Women providing food to their families and communities do not have "jobs," yet they work more and harder than anyone else.

Generating meaningful and productive work and creating employment, including self-employment, are all outputs in an ecological system of production. Reducing human activity to labor, and transforming it from an output to an input, is a prescription for unemployment, displacement, and the destruction of livelihoods of small family farmers and their communities the world over.

The devaluing of livelihoods is also a recipe for further intensifying the external inputs of chemicals and fossil fuels, which rather than feeding people and sustaining farming systems, create hunger and generate environmental degradation. This is known as the "myth of more," in which an agricultural system where a farmer spends more for costs of inputs than she or he will earn from selling a monoculture commodity is presented as "productive," a path to higher incomes and higher production. The reality that undercuts this myth is that through globalized trade, genetically engineered seeds, and corporate-owed farms, farmers' incomes are actually declining, leading to debt, displacement, and the suicides of farmers.

According to the Indian Ministry of Agriculture, which has vested interests in corporate, large-scale agriculture,

> Limited land holding per capita in India is a great obstacle which inhibits large scale mechanisation and adopting other measures for increasing the productivity and bringing down the unit cost of production. It is a well known fact that in the major exporting countries like USA, Canada, and Australia, the cost of production is low since the farms are fully mechanised, little human labour is used, and natural resources such as soil fertility and rainfall distribution are better.[1]

But in developed countries, only 15 percent of the price of a loaf of bread goes to the farmer—the rest goes to milling, baking, packaging, transportation, and marketing. For agribusiness, high production costs and low commodity prices translate into two-way profits. For the farmer, they translate into a negative economy and spiraling debts. Even though US farm exports from large monocultures are booming, farmers cannot survive. More US farmers die of suicides than of any other unnatural cause. As a group, farmers are three times more likely to kill themselves than the general population.[2]

In 2000, the Canadian National Farmers Union submitted a report to the Senate called "The Farm Crisis." The report reads:

> While the farmers growing cereal grains—wheat, oats, corn—earn negative returns and are pushed close to bankruptcy, the companies that make breakfast cereals reap huge profits. In 1998, cereal companies Kellogg's, Quaker Oats, and General Mills enjoyed return on equity rates of 56%, 165%, and 222% respectively. While a bushel of corn sold for less than $4, a bushel of corn flakes sold for $133. In 1998, the cereal companies were 186 to 740 times more profitable than the farms. Maybe farmers are making too little because others are taking too much.[3]

A false logic is established through the "myth of more," according to which industrial monocultures produce more, and more food leads to lower prices. But when viewed in terms of total food output—rather than marketable commodity output—large-scale farming does not produce more. As we shall see in Chapter Seven, low prices, as in the case of wheat cereal, are linked to monopoly control rather than more food production. The lowering of agricultural prices is not due to an increase in productivity or efficiency, but to agribusiness, which takes several times more from the land than it gives back to either the farmer or the Earth.

The Indian Ministry of Agriculture would do well to learn from the successes of its own food production prior to the implementation of Green Revolution, large-scale monocultures. As former Indian Prime Minister Charan Singh once stated,

> Agriculture being a life process, in actual practice, under given conditions, yields per acre decline as the size of farm increases (in other words, as the application of human labour and supervision per acre decreases). The above results are well-nigh universal: output per acre of investment is higher on small farms than on large farms. Thus, if

a crowded, capital-scarce country like India has a choice between a single 100 acre farm and forty 2.5 acre farms, the capital cost to the national economy will be less if the country chooses the small farms.[4]

Small farms produce more food than large industrial farms because small-scale farmers give more care to the soil, plants, and animals, and they intensify biodiversity, not external chemical inputs. As farms increase in size, they replace labor with fossil fuels for farm machinery, the caring work of farmers with toxic chemicals, and the intelligence of nature and farmers with careless technologies.

However, when profit is the name of the (food) game, it is the small farms and small-scale farmers who are being destroyed by globalization and trade-driven economic reforms. Five million peasants' livelihoods have disappeared in India since agricultural "reforms" were introduced. And in fifteen years, 284,000 farmers have committed suicide because of the nonsustainability of capital- and chemical-intensive farming based on nonrenewable seeds.[5]

Today, it is time to break the "myth of more" and give credit where it is due: not to global agribusiness, but to small-scale farmers across the world, who, despite all the threats they face, put food on our tables.

Small is big when it comes to food. In spite of all subsidies going to large farms, and in spite of all the governmental policies that promote industrial agriculture, today 70 percent of the world's food comes from small farms, according to the UN Food and Agriculture Organization (FAO). If we add kitchen gardens and urban gardens, it becomes clear that most food that people eat is grown on a small scale. What is growing on large farms is not food; it is commodities. For example, only 10 percent of the corn and soy taking over world agriculture is eaten. Ninety percent goes to drive cars as biofuel, or to feed animals being tortured in factory farms.

Under the Law of Exploitation fostered by a reductive, militaristic knowledge and science paradigm, food is produced in linear chains, which hide ecological nonsustainability and social injustice. The common corporate language is one of value chains. The food web is converted into a food chain, and cycles that renew and rejuvenate are now converted into linear flows of exploitation. When the value returned to the farmer is reduced to grow corporate profits, it is called value added. When industrial processing takes away nutrition and quality from food, it is called value added. In the food chain, value removed is presented as value added.

The Law of Return, on the other hand, is based on cycles that exist in a web of relationships. This web gives back to the Earth, to society, and to farmers. While food chains are used to justify exploitation and violence, food webs are the basis of sustainability and justice. Food chains are controlled by corporate greed, while food webs are sustained by small farms and small-scale farmers. This can be seen across the world.

Peasants and small-scale farmers, especially women, account for more than half of Russia's agricultural production, but occupy only a quarter of the agricultural lands. In Ukraine, small-scale farmers produce 55 percent of the country's agricultural output on only 16 percent of the land, while in Kazakhstan, where they occupy half the land, they account for 73 percent of agricultural production. The fact is that these countries are fed by their peasants and by their small-scale farmers. And this is true the world over. Wherever official data is available, including for the European Union, Colombia, and Brazil, or where studies have been undertaken, including countries in Asia, Africa, and Latin America, peasant farming is shown to be more efficient than large-scale agribusiness.[6]

Take, for instance, some of these examples:

- In Papua New Guinea, as many as five thousand varieties of sweet potato are cultivated, with more than twenty varieties grown in a single garden.
- In Java, small-scale farmers cultivate 607 species in their home gardens, with an overall species diversity comparable to that in a deciduous tropical forest.

- A single home garden in Thailand has more than 230 species.
- In eastern Nigeria, home gardens occupying only 2 percent of a household's farmland account for half of the farm's total output.
- Home gardens in Indonesia are estimated to provide more than 20 percent of household income and 40 percent of domestic food supplies.[7]

The central argument used for the industrialization of food and the corporatization of agriculture is the low productivity of the small-scale farmer. Surely these families and farmers, on their little plots of land, are capable of meeting the world's need for food?

The UNCTAD (United Nations Conference on Trade and Development)'s 2013 *Trade and Environment Review*[8] shows that monoculture and industrial farming methods are not providing sufficient, affordable food where it is needed, while also causing mounting and unsustainable environmental damage. It goes on to state that farming in rich and poor nations alike should shift from large-scale, chemical, globalized monocultures toward greater varieties of crops, a reduced use of fertilizers and other inputs, greater support for small-scale farmers, and more locally focused production and consumption of food. Similarly, the FAO's analysis shows that small farms can be thousands of times more productive than large farms.[9]

An ILO (International Labour Organization) report[10] shows that small-scale agriculture is the solution to the ecological crisis, the food crisis, and the crisis of work and employment. The report cites examples of how small farms in Africa have increased food production through ecological agriculture. A project involving one thousand farmers in South Nyanza, Kenya, who are cultivating two hectares each on average, showed that their crop yields rose by 2–4 metric tons per hectare after an initial conversion to organic farming. In yet another case, the incomes of thirty thousand smallholders in Thika, Kenya, rose by 50 percent within three years. The International Assessment of Agricultural Knowledge, Science and Technology for Development has also confirmed that small ecological farms are a more effective solution to world hunger than the Green Revolution or genetic engineering.

Navdanya's studies in India also point to an increase in farmers' incomes through small-scale, biodiverse farming. The four crops being externally imposed on Indian farmers today are GMO Bt cotton, hybrid rice, hybrid corn, and soy. Farmers growing organic cotton, indigenous rice, millets, and indigenous pulses earn more in a just trade system than farmers selling their produce through commodity trade. Farmers growing hybrid rice earn Rs. 71,862/hectare, whereas Navdanya member Mukundi Lal, growing organic indigenous basmati rice, earns Rs. 113,031/hectare. Farmers growing soy earn Rs. 2,863/hectare, whereas farmers like Mohan Singh of Chakrata, growing indigenous kidney beans, earn Rs. 267,399/hectare. Farmers growing hybrid corn earn Rs. 30,657/hectare, whereas Rajeshwari of Rudraprayag, who grows finger millet (*ragi*), earns Rs. 219,400/hectare, and Susheela Devi, who conserves and grows amaranth, earns Rs. 367,000/hectare. Conserving biodiversity and practicing agroecology on small farms have undeniably enhanced farmers' incomes.

Small-scale farmers are not just producers of food and nutrition. They are custodians of seed and soil, conservators of water and land, and protectors and rejuvenators of biological and cultural diversity. They produce more using less, and are hence more productive and efficient than the large industrial monocultures they are being replaced with. From less than 30 percent of the world's arable land, small-scale farmers produce 70 percent of the food eaten in the world. Agribusiness, on the other hand, uses 70 percent of the world's arable land to produce a mere 30 percent of the food.

So who *really* feeds the world? The numbers speak loud and clear.

———

Today, small-scale farmers are in crisis. They are being wiped out by the rules of corporate globalization, designed to maximize corporate profits at the cost of small-scale farmers. Corporations sell costly inputs in the form of seeds and chemicals to farmers, and buy their produce at cheap prices. Farmers are locked into debt, and farming is made unviable, leading to a massive exodus from the countryside to urban slums. Since the policies of globalization of agriculture were introduced in 1991, farmers have shrunk in number from 110 million to 95.8 million. That is a loss of nearly fifteen million farmers, or two thousand farmers per day.

Through aggressive landgrabs, farmers are losing their land. The overall amount of agricultural land across the world is shrinking, but it is also becoming increasingly concentrated in a few large shareholdings in the hands of even fewer large private entities. In the European Union, the top 1 percent of farms control 20 percent of EU farmland, and the top 3 percent of farms control 50 percent of EU farmland. Eighty percent of farms, presumably made up of small-scale farmers, control just 14.5 percent of all farming land. The movement to large-scale farming has rapidly displaced farmers, and between 2007 and 2010, small-scale farmers owning less than ten hectares lost control of 17 percent of Europe's farmland—an area bigger than Switzerland, whereas farmers and companies owning more than fifty hectares gained almost seven million hectares in the same period—an area twice the size of Belgium.[11]

In the United States, farmland is moving out of the hands of farmers, either because they are "too old" to farm or because they have been forced to mortgage their land. Corporations are starting to buy up farmland, especially in areas dominated by large-scale industrial agriculture. According to a USDA report, 40 percent of farmland in the United States is rented by farmers from banks and investors. In states that are major industrial agriculture centers, including Iowa, Illinois, and California, the figure is as high as 50 percent.[12]

In India, landgrabs for mines, highways, and sprawling cities have uprooted peasants and tribal people from their farmers, farms, and homes. According to the Indian Ministry of Agriculture, India lost 16,000 km^2 (0.8 percent) of its farmland area in the ten-year period leading up to 2010–2011. Much of this loss was at the expense of rural land and was added to cities, and the Indian Census Commissioner calculates that for the same time period, the area under urban use jumped by 24,000 km^2.[13] As cities grow, neighboring agricultural areas shrink. The 284,000 farmer suicides in India are linked to debt-induced landgrabs. Farmers are being trapped into debt as corporations push costly seeds and chemicals under the illusory promise that farmers will earn more. When creditors come to take the land—because instead of farmers getting richer, they became indebted—farmers drink pesticide to end their lives.

The assumption that big feeds the world and not small is leading to the destruction of the foundations of farming and of community that feed us, and thus destroying our food security base.

It is time for the living economies of the small to join with the living democracies of the small to create peace, harmony, abundance, and well-being for all. Gandhi responded to the bigness of the British Empire by pulling out the spinning wheel, hand-spinning his own clothes, and thereby rejecting machine-spun textiles imported from England, which themselves relied on cotton exports from India. In doing so, he sparked the Swadeshi movement, encouraging countless Indians to follow his example and reclaim textile production on a small scale. This small scale had big, rippling effects. As Gandhi said, "Anything that millions can do together becomes charged with unique power.... The wheel as such is lifeless, but when I invest it with symbolism, it becomes a living thing for me."[14]

Inspired by Gandhi's spinning wheel, I started Navdanya for saving seeds and promoting organic farming during an era when giant corporations are concentrating their control on the seed and on our food. Working with small-scale farmers, we are creating food security, livelihood security, and ecological security. Connecting the small seed and the small-scale farmers in ever-expanding circles of cooperation, we are creating a paradigm shift to an old understanding that must be made new again: small is big.

The seed is small, but it is also the powerhouse of life and freedom. Each of us can be savers of seed and growers of living food, and we can support the millions of small-scale farmers and growers across the world who put food on our plates and inject life into the earth. Recently, and despite the FAO's findings, its director general, José Graziano da Silva, coauthored an article with Suma Chakrabarti, the president of the European Bank for Reconstruction and Development (EBRD), where they called upon people to "fertilize this land with money."[15] But it is organic matter, living organisms, and the love, care, and intelligence of small-scale farmers that fertilize the soil, not money.

In Rumi's words

> *in this earth*
> *in this earth*
> *in this immaculate field*
> *we shall not plant any seeds*
> *except for compassion*
> *except for love*

6

Seed Freedom Feeds the World,
Not Seed Dictatorship

We don't sell seed; we sell profit.

—SHRIRAM BIOSEED GENETICS CORPORATE
LITERATURE

Seed is the first link in the food chain and the repository of life's future evolution: it is the very foundation of our being. Seeds have evolved freely over millennia and given us diversity and richness of life on the planet. For thousands of years, farmers, and especially women, have evolved and bred seed freely in partnership with each other and with nature. Farmers' seeds carry within them the knowledge of an agroecological, connected web of food and life.

In the last half century, a reductionist, mechanistic paradigm has laid down the legal and economic framework for privatizing seeds and the knowledge of seeds. This has destroyed diversity, denied farmers' innovation and breeding rights, enclosed the biological and intellectual commons through patents, and created seed monopolies.

This destruction has been made possible by a systemic discrediting of farmers' native seed varieties. These seeds have been developed by farmers over centuries to suit their ecological, nutritional, taste, medicinal, fodder, fuel, and other needs. But because corporations want to control, adapt, and genetically modify seeds for their own profit, farmers' varieties are being called "primitive cultivars" and are contrasted with "elite cultivars," or those seeds evolved by scientists, or the "elite."

This "elite" knowledge is reducing farmers' varieties to a genetic meme, which can then be stolen, extracted, and patented by large companies. Not only is the negation of farmers' breeding unfair and unjust to farmers, it is unfair and unjust to society as a whole, because farmers' varieties have taste, nutrition, and quality. That is why wherever heirloom or traditional varieties have been saved and cultivated, people prefer them to hybrids and GMOs.

These indigenous farmers' varieties can be saved and replanted year after year. Globally, more than 1.4 billion people depend on farm-saved seed as their primary seed source.[1] In order for agribusinesses to make profits, they must rupture this self-sustaining, nutritious system of food production. Farmers' varieties are therefore being replaced by three new seed varieties: high yielding varieties (HYVs), hybrid seeds, and GMOs.

HYVs, as we have seen, are in fact high *response* varieties, and are heavily dependent on chemicals and fertilizers. HYVs are also vulnerable to disease and pests, so although farmers may initially be able to save them, they need to be replaced after one or two crops. To do this, farmers have to buy new seeds.

Hybrid seeds are first-generation seeds produced from crossing two genetically dissimilar parent species. The progeny of these seeds cannot be saved or replanted, because the next generations will give much lower yields. Hybrid seeds force farmers to go to the market every season. Hybrid seeds lay the foundations for the biological patenting of the seed. No one else, neither farmer nor rival company, can produce the exact same seeds unless they know the parent lines, which are company secrets. Combined with the introduction of new laws, this biological patenting effectively prevents the farmer from multiplying, saving, and selling seeds.[2]

GMOs, or genetically engineered organisms, are made by using the technique of gene splicing or recombinant DNA to introduce genes from an unrelated organism into the cells of a plant. This is done by one of two methods: using a gene gun to shoot the gene, or introducing a plant cancer called agrobacterium to infect the plant. Since both techniques are unreliable, an antibiotic-resistance gene is added to separate the cells that absorbed the new gene from those that did not. Further, since the gene is not part of the plant genome, there is a tendency for the plant to not express the traits for which the gene was introduced. For this, genes of virulent viruses are added as promoters so the plant is more likely to express the traits. In this way, every GMO has four characteristics: genes that do not belong to the plant, genes for plant cancer, genes for antibiotic-resistance markers, and the genes of viruses that act as promoters. This bundle of genes causes harm to the plant, to biodiversity, and to those who eat it.

Another newer type of GMO is the terminator seed. Terminator seeds are genetically engineered seeds that release a lethal toxin that kills the embryo of the seed, making it sterile. Monsanto owns the patent on terminator technology together with the US Department of Agriculture. There was an attempt to commercialize terminator technology a few years ago, but a global campaign, of which I was a part, had a moratorium put on these seeds through the UN Convention on Biological Diversity.

Corporations say that GMOs are substantially equivalent to non-GMO crops and food, but the same corporations also simultaneously claim that GMOs are new and different, that they are inventions. Under this logic, the same GMO is natural when it comes to avoiding responsibility for safety, but it is different from the natural—or unnatural—when it comes to owning it. This is ontological schizophrenia. GMOs have been introduced with only one purpose: to own seeds and life-forms through patents. In this way, GMOs become both a source of control and a source of profits through royalty collection.

The diversity of farmers' seeds has been rendered invisible in a process that began with the Green Revolution. Instilling the assumption that farmers' seed varieties are "empty," today Green Revolution agriculture is continued through corporate industrial breeding that continues to give us seeds and crops that are not only nutritionally empty, but also loaded with toxins.

The shift to HYVs, hybrid seeds, and GMOs has meant that from once being a free resource reproduced on farms, seeds have been transformed into costly inputs that farmers now need to purchase. Countries have been forced to take international loans to help spread the new seeds, and farmers have had to obtain credit from banks to use them. International agricultural centers—like the CIMMYT (International Maize and Wheat Improvement Center) in Mexico, and the IRRI (International Rice Research Institute) in the Philippines, which later became part of the World Bank–run centers of agricultural research—are launching pads for these new seeds.[3]

Twenty years ago there were thousands of seed companies, most of which were small and family owned. Today, the top ten global seed companies control one-third of the $23 billion in the commercial seed trade.[4] Multinational seed companies are seeking absolute control of seed, and through control over seed, control over the food system. If all farmers, who are the original breeders, could be forced into the market every year, the seed industry would have a market worth trillions of dollars.

Every seed is an embodiment of millennia of nature's evolution and centuries of farmers' breeding. It is the distilled expression of the intelligence of the Earth and the intelligence of farming communities. Farmers have bred seeds for diversity, resilience, taste, nutrition, health, and adaption to local agroecosystems.

On the other hand, industrial breeding treats nature's contributions and farmers' contributions as nothing. Just as the jurisprudence of *terra nullius* defined the land as empty and allowed mass colonization by imperial European countries, the jurisprudence of intellectual property rights related to life-forms is *bio nullius:* life as empty of intelligence. The Earth is defined as dead matter, so it cannot create. And farmers have empty heads, so they cannot breed plants.

Peruvian anthropologist and poet José María Arguedas writes in "A Call to Certain Academics":

> They say that we do not know anything. That we are backwardness. That our head needs changing for a better one. They say that some learned men are saying this about us. These academics who reproduce themselves in our own lives. What is there on the banks of these rivers, Doctor? Take out your binoculars and your spectacles. Look if you can. Five hundred flowers from five hundred different types of potato grow on the terraces above abysses that your eyes don't reach. Those five hundred flowers are my brain, my flesh.[5]

In a bid to lay the groundwork for *bio nullius* through the Law of Domination and the Law of Exploitation, corporations are declaring themselves to be the "creators" of seed. By doing so, they claim seeds as their "invention," and hence something that they can now patent. A patent is an exclusive right granted for an invention, which allows the patent holder to exclude everyone else from making, selling, distributing, and using the patented product. With patents on seed, the farmers' right to save and share seed is now defined as "theft," or an "intellectual property crime."

The door to patents on seed and patents on life was opened by genetic engineering. By adding one new gene to the cell of a plant, corporations claimed they had invented and created the seed, and the plant, and that all future seeds were their property. Under this logic, GMO came to mean God Move Over. While GMOs are presented as just another technology, they are the tool for creating a global system of control over our seed and food.

Large corporations defined farmers' acts of saving seed as a problem, which needed to be "fixed" by preventing farmers from seed saving and seed sharing. In order to do this, corporations began advocating for global intellectual property rights following the "success" of the Green Revolution. This is how the Trade-Related Aspects of Intellectual Property Rights (TRIPS) Agreement of the World Trade Organization was born in 1994.

Article 27.3(b) of the TRIPS Agreement states:

> Parties may exclude from patentability plants and animals other than micro-organisms, and essentially biological processes for the production of plants or animals other than non-biological and micro-biological processes. However, parties shall provide for the protection of plant varieties either by patents or by an effective *sui generis system or by any combination thereof.*[6]

This protection of plant varieties is precisely what prohibits the free exchange of seeds between farmers. Monsanto—one of the five big seed giants and the *only* corporation that has commercialized GMOs—acknowledges its role in drafting the TRIPS Agreement. In fact, a Monsanto representative once infamously stated that they were the "patient, diagnostician, [and] physician" all in one. The "disease" they diagnosed and sought to cure was that farmers saved seeds. The "cure" was that farmers should be prevented from saving and exchanging seeds by defining these fundamental freedoms as a crime. Simply put, TRIPS imposes patents on seeds, and patents allow corporations like Monsanto to prevent farmers from saving seeds. Today, Monsanto has patented 1,676 seeds, plants, and other applicable processes across the world.[7]

In 2007 Monsanto sued Vernon Hugh Bowman, an American farmer from Indiana, for reproducing patented seeds. But Bowman never bought Monsanto seeds; he used to buy his seeds from other farmers in what are known as grain elevators. As it turns out, some of these seeds were transgenic: they had a Monsanto gene in them. Bowman fought the case until 2013 all the way up to the Supreme Court, which finally ruled in favor of Monsanto. This ruling describes the grain that comes out of the seed as Monsanto's property, which in effect means that farmers cannot buy grain from the market and grow a crop from it without paying Monsanto.

Worse still, we find the case of Percy Schmeiser, a Canadian farmer whose canola crop was genetically contaminated by Monsanto's Roundup Ready canola. This was discovered after Monsanto sent private detectives into his fields, and rather than paying the farmer for biological pollution, Monsanto sued Schmeiser for $200,000, accusing him of "stealing" their property. Schmeiser fought Monsanto on the grounds that it was Monsanto's genes that had corrupted *his* crops. In 2004 the court ruled in favor of Monsanto, though it gave Schmeiser a partial victory by stating that he did not have to pay the seed giant because there was no evidence he had profited from the contamination of his crops.

These two rulings have grave consequences. In the case of Bowman, the court's ruling sets a precedent for Monsanto and others to *own all future generations of seeds* (because it is, of course, in the nature of seed to reproduce). In the case of Schmeiser, the ruling means that companies like Monsanto can use patents to sue farmers whose crops it has contaminated. In other words, *contamination makes it theirs.* Alarmingly, Monsanto also sponsors a toll-free "tip line" in North America to help farmers blow the whistle on other farmers whose crops may be contaminated or who may have purchased seeds from a source other than Monsanto.[8] As Hope Shand of the Rural Advancement Foundation International says, "Our rural communities are being turned into corporate police states, and farmers are being turned into criminals."[9]

Now the United States is pushing TRIPS onto developing countries on behalf of Monsanto, and genetic contamination is spreading. India has lost her native cotton because of contamination from Monsanto's Bt cotton. Mexico, the historical cradle of corn, has lost 80 percent of its corn varieties. These are only two instances of the loss of local and national seed heritage. After contamination, as in the case of Schmeiser, biotech seed corporations sue farmers for patent infringement. Recently, more than eighty groups came together to file a case in the United States to prevent Monsanto from suing farmers whose seed had been contaminated.

The TRIPS clause on patents on life was due for a mandatory review in 1999. In its submission, India stated, "Clearly, there is a case for re-examining the need to grant patents on life forms anywhere in the world. Until such systems are in place, it may be advisable to ... exclude patents on all life forms."[10]

In a similar vein, the African Group stated the following:

> For plant varieties to be protected under the TRIPS Agreement, the protection must clearly, and not just implicitly or by way of exception, strike a good balance with the interests of the community as a whole and protect farmers' rights and traditional knowledge, and ensure the preservation of biological diversity.[11]

But this mandatory review has been subverted by the United States, which has prevented review discussions from taking place.

Simultaneously, the US government has been threatening countries, including India, to change their laws to recognize that Monsanto creates seeds. But seed creates itself; all Monsanto does is add a toxic gene. Monsanto should be recognized as a polluter, except as examples from across the world have shown, this logic has been grossly perverted.

So far, they have not been successful in reversing existing laws in India. On July 5, 2013, the Indian courts denied Monsanto's attempt to patent the climate-resilient features of plants. The courts used Article 3(j) of the Indian Patents Act, which excludes from patentability

> plants and animals in whole or any part thereof other than micro-organisms but including seeds, varieties and species and essentially biological processes for production or propagation of plants and animals.

In other words, the ruling showed that life and its biological processes (re)produce themselves and cannot be deemed as manufactured or assembled by an external force.

Today, in addition to patents, new seed laws are being enforced across the world so that corporations can make farmers' seeds and local diverse varieties illegal. These are laws of uniformity, enforced either through UPOV—the International Union for the Protection of New Varieties of Plants, which allows intellectual property rights on plants in seventy-one member countries—or through seed acts that require seed registration.

In 2004 an attempt was made to introduce a seed law in India, which would have required the compulsory registration of farmers' varieties. In response, we started a Seed Satyagraha, and the law has not yet been passed. Satyagraha means "force of truth" and was a word used by Gandhi to encourage noncooperation with unjust laws. In Gandhi's words, "As long as the superstition exists that unjust law must be obeyed, so long will slavery exist."

But there are many examples of how seed acts and intellectual property rights prevent farmers across the world from engaging in their own seed production. Take Josef Albrecht, an organic farmer in Germany, who was not satisfied with commercially available seed. He developed his own ecological varieties of wheat, and ten other organic farmers from neighboring villages took his wheat seeds. For saving, sharing, and planting his own seeds, the government fined Albrecht because he had traded in uncertified seed.

In Scotland, there are a large number of potato farmers. They could, until the early 1990s, freely sell seeds to other potato growers, merchants, or farmers. In the 1990s, holders of plant breeders' rights started to issue notices to potato growers through the British Society of Plant Breeders, and made the selling of seed potato to other farmers illegal. In February 1995, the society decided to proceed with a high-profile court case against an Aberdeenshire farmer. The farmer was forced to pay £30,000 as compensation to cover royalties lost by the seed industry as a result of direct farmer-to-farmer exchange. Currently, laws in the United Kingdom and the European Union prevent seed exchange of any type.[12]

Seed laws for compulsory registration that are being pushed everywhere are based on the illegitimate restriction of people's freedom in order to enhance corporate freedom and establish seed monopolies.

Corporations are also manipulating governments across the world to introduce pseudosafety and pseudohygiene laws that make safe food illegal and declare hazardous food as safe. The Prevention of Food Adulteration Act of India was replaced by a Food Safety and Standards Act, which is now criminalizing street vendors, small neighborhood eating stalls, and farmers, while deregulating the biotechnology and industrial food industries. I have called it the "Food Fascism Act." In the United States, the Food Safety Modernization Act is doing the same thing. Organic farmer Joel Salatin wrote a book aptly titled *Everything I Want to Do Is Illegal: War Stories from the Local Food Front,* describing this shift in priorities from real food to commodities.

The corporate control over seed is first and foremost a form of violence against farmers. While farmers breed for diversity, corporations breed for uniformity. While farmers breed for resilience, corporations breed for vulnerability. While farmers breed for taste, quality, and nutrition, industries breed for industrial processing and long-distance transportation in a globalized food system. Monocultures of industrial crops and monocultures of industrial junk food reinforce each other, wasting the land, wasting food, and wasting our health.

The privileging of uniformity over diversity and of quantity over quality of nutrition has degraded our diets and displaced the rich biodiversity of our food and crops. It is based on a false "creation boundary" that excludes nature's intelligence and creativity and farmers' intelligence and creativity. It has created a legal boundary to disenfranchise farmers of their seed freedom and seed sovereignty and to impose unjust seed laws that establish corporate monopolies on seed. An arsenal of legal instruments is being invented and imposed undemocratically to criminalize farmers' seed breeding, seed saving, and seed sharing. This is violence against farmers, which has manifested primarily in three ways.

First, their contribution to breeding is erased, and what farmers have coevolved with nature is patented as an innovation. We call this biopiracy. Patents on life are a hijacking of biodiversity and indigenous knowledge; they are instruments of monopoly control over life itself. Patents on living resources and indigenous knowledge are an enclosure of the biological and intellectual commons. Life-forms have been redefined as "manufactured" and "machines," robbing life of its integrity and self-organization. Traditional knowledge is being pirated and patented, and through biopiracy, Western corporations claim indigenous biodiversity and farmers' varieties as their "inventions." Examples of this from India can be seen in the patents on neem, turmeric, and basmati rice. To save the sovereignty and rights of farmers, our legal systems must recognize the rights of communities and their collective and cumulative innovation in breeding diversity, and not merely the rights of corporations.

Second, patents lead to royalty collection, and royalty collection is extortion in the name of technology and improvement. In Brazil, farmers have been fighting against seed giant Monsanto, most recently filing a lawsuit suing the company for more than $6 million on the grounds that the company has been unfairly collecting royalties from farmers. The seeds on which Monsanto has been collecting royalties are from what are known as "renewal" seed harvests, which means that these seeds have been collected from the previous harvest: a practice used for centuries. But because these seeds are from Monsanto's genetically modified plants, Monsanto is demanding that farmers pay. Not only are these royalties unfairly enforced, they are pushing farmers deeper into debt that they cannot pay back, leaving them floundering in their fields of failed genetically modified crops.

Third, when genetically engineered crops contaminate neighboring farmers' fields, the "polluter pay" principle is turned on its head. Corporations use patents to establish the principle of "polluter gets paid." This is what happened in the case of Percy Schmeiser in Canada, as well as to thousands of farmers in the United States.

If the first colonization based on *terra nullius* gave us landlords, who pushed two million people to death during the Great Bengal famine of 1943, the new bio imperialism based on *bio nullius* has given us life lords: the biotechnology/seed/chemical industry, which has pushed thousands of farmers across the world to suicide.

In 2003, Lee Kyung Hae, a Korean farmer, took his life at the barricades of the people's protest against the World Trade Organization (WTO), an organization that has been instrumental in liberalizing and privatizing seed. As he stabbed himself, he carried a banner reading, "WTO Kills Farmers." Mr. Lee's suicide was symbolic of the suicides of thousands of farmers across the globe as a result of corporate seed control.

The inability to repay past debt—and therefore to access fresh loans—has been widely accepted as the most significant proximate cause of the farmers' suicides that are widespread in different areas in India. Since 1995, 284,000 farmers in India have killed themselves[13] due to rising input prices and volatile output prices. As governmental support for farmers declined through liberalization, and as breeders could no longer access credit from public-sector or cooperative banks, they were driven into the hands of potentially more exploitative, usurious relationships. While institutional credit would have left farmers' land intact, farmers were instead forced to borrow from either traditional moneylenders or, worse, agents of the seed and chemical companies, who would give credit against the farmers' land. And the day the farmer loses the land is the day the farmer commits suicide.

Farming communities are increasingly losing their family members, who have been driven to death by increased costs of seeds, increased debts, and crop failures. There have been several cases in which farmers have had to sell their land and even their kidneys to pay off their loans. In other cases, their houses or tractors have been mortgaged to the loan providers, or they have been arrested when they failed to pay back the loans.

Navdanya has been updating a report entitled *Seeds of Suicide* since 1997, which shows how farmers' suicides in India—and across the world—are the result of policies of market freedom. Liberalization, privatization, and globalization trends in agriculture have resulted in the creation of an unregulated seed industry. At the same time, existing rules and regulations have been either abandoned or modified to accommodate multinational and transnational corporations. Farmers' seed supply and direct-exchange networks have been adversely affected by the proliferation of unregulated seed markets.[14]

For me, every life is equal, whether it is the life of a US citizen or an Indian farmer. However, those who justify the deaths of farmers across the globe as the collateral damage in improving the economy should consider the fallacy of their argument. If the United States' accident and health insurance measure for the value of life is applied to the cost of farmers' suicides to the Indian economy, the figure would be 5 percent of the GDP. For the 284,000 farmers' suicides since 1995, this translates to $1.99 trillion.

Farmers are the original breeders, and farmers' rights to seed are a fundamental right to food and livelihoods. Yet Monsanto and other companies have created a system where those who have been custodians and givers of seed are now being criminalized. In extreme cases such as in India, they are being pushed to end their lives. Seed, which is the source of life, has been appropriated and privatized to cause the end of life for farmers. This is genocide.

Today, the freedom of nature and culture to evolve is under violent and direct threat. The worldview of *bio nullius* unleashes violence and injustice on the Earth, on farmers, and on all citizens. We are losing biodiversity and cultural diversity, and we are losing nutrition, taste, and quality in our food. Above all, we are losing our fundamental freedom to decide what seeds we will sow, how we will grow our food, and what we will eat. The seed is the first point of attack, but conversely, it is also our first line of defense. It is where we begin the fight for seed freedom.

We use the term "seed freedom" to talk about the right of the seed as a living, self-organized system that can evolve freely without the threat of extinction, genetic contamination, or termination through technologies designed to make seeds sterile. Seed freedom is the freedom of bees to pollinate freely, without threat of extinction due to poisons. Seed freedom is the freedom of the web of life to weave itself in integrity and resilience, fostering interconnectedness and well-being for all. Seed freedom is the right of farmers to save, exchange, breed, and sell farmers' varieties—seeds that have been evolved over millennia—without interference by the state or by corporations. Seed freedom is the freedom of eaters to have access to food grown from seeds bred for diversity, taste, flavor, quality, and nutrition.

Seed freedom is the duty to save and exchange native seeds bred by farmers. This is also seed sovereignty. For farmers' varieties to be conserved, used, and bred as a commons, this will entail self-organization and self-rule at the level of local communities, free from interference by the state or corporations. At national and international levels, seed freedom includes the obligation of governments to protect the freedoms of biodiversity and people by regulating corporations to prevent them from undermining people's sovereignty through biopiracy on the one hand, and threats to biosafety from genetically engineered seeds and crops on the other. Seed freedom and seed sovereignty is to have the freedom to self-govern at the level of the community, to take care of the commons, and to share sustainably and equitably in its fruits. It also involves freedom from harm through national and international regulations.

Seed freedom means regulation by the state of those who can cause harm to others, thus creating the context for the practice of freedom in people's spaces. This is how rapists do not have the freedom to rape, murderers do not have the freedom to murder, and polluters do not have the freedom to pollute. Corporations, on the other hand, have unprecedented capacities to harm the Earth and its people with new technologies like genetic engineering. This must be stopped now.

For me, saving and protecting life on Earth, especially biodiversity and seeds, is the highest *dharma,* or duty. In 1987, when I heard the corporations spell out their vision of total control over life through genetic engineering and patents on life and seeds, I started Navdanya. Navdanya was formed to protect our seed diversity and farmers' rights to save, breed, and exchange seed freely. For me, life-forms, plants, and seeds are all evolving, self-organized, sovereign beings. They have intrinsic worth, value, and standing. Owning life by claiming it to be a corporate invention is ethically and legally wrong. Patents on seeds are legally wrong, because seeds are not an invention. Patents on seeds are ethically wrong, because seeds are life-forms—they are kin members of our Earth Family.

In 2001, the Agriculture Minister at the time, Shri Chaturanan Mishra, invited me to be a part of the expert group for drafting a law entitled The Protection of Plant Varieties and Farmers' Rights Act. Within this law we were able to include a clause for farmers' rights, which states

> a farmer shall be deemed to be entitled to save, use, sow, resow, exchange, share or sell his farm produce including seed of a variety protected under this Act in the same manner as he was entitled before the coming into force of this Act.

Resistance to unjust seed laws through the Seed Satyagraha is one aspect of seed freedom. Saving and sharing seeds is another aspect. That is why Navdanya has worked with local communities to reclaim seed diversity and seed as a commons, by establishing more than one hundred community seed banks. Across the world, communities are saving and exchanging seeds in diverse ways, appropriate to their contexts. They are creating and re-creating freedom—for the seed, for seed keepers, and for all life.

In 2012, climate movements and scientists across the world put together a participatory report, sparking a global Seed Freedom Movement. The organizations and movements coming together in this initiative include Shumei International, Kokopelli (France), Slow Food International, ETC Group, GRAIN (International), Nayakrishi (Bangladesh), African Centre for Biosafety, African Biodiversity Network, IFOAM (International Federation of Organic Agriculture Movements), Grupo de Reflexión Rural (Argentina), Center for Food Safety (United States), OSGATA (Organic Seed Growers and Trade Association, United States), Perennia (Canada), No Patents on Seeds, Arche Noah (Austria), Associazione Donne in Campo (Italy), Fondation Danielle Mitterrand (France), and Red Semillas Libres (Chile).

The movement brings together activists, scientists, and citizens to respond to the seed emergency by alerting people and governments to how precarious our seed supply has become. Since its inception, the movement has already reached more than five million people in various countries in a bid to reclaim seeds as a commons and protect the biodiversity of our planet. The Seed Freedom Movement is a small seed we hope will multiply and reproduce until no seed, no farmer, and no citizen is bonded, colonized, or enslaved. The stories of seed freedom are stories of courageous and creative individuals and organizations that are challenging unjust laws.

Across the world, various seed movements are defending the freedom of seeds, farmers, and citizens. In India, a Bija Satyagraha stopped the introduction of a seed law in 2004 that would have made farmers' seeds illegal. In Europe, when the European Commission tried to introduce a seed law that would have criminalized biodiversity and local seed varieties, the Seed Freedom Movement worked with the European Parliament, and the law was sent back to the European Commission. In Colombia, farmers took to the streets to stop a seed law that would make their seeds illegal. I traveled across Africa in 2014 to support the indigenous movements for seed sovereignty and food sovereignty.

In every country there is a contest between people's movements for seed freedom and the corporate push for seed dictatorship. Food democracy rests on seed freedom. Seed dictatorship is the foundation for food dictatorship. During the Vietnam War, Henry Kissinger said, "Food is a weapon." Today, seed has become the ultimate weapon in a war against the Earth and her people. In this war, if corporations win, we will all lose our food and our future.

Seed freedom has become an ecological, political, economic, and cultural imperative. If we do not respond, or if we have a fragmented and weak response, species will irreversibly disappear. Agriculture, including the food and cultural spectrum dependent on biodiversity, will disappear. Small-scale farmers will disappear, healthy food diversity will disappear, seed sovereignty will disappear, and food sovereignty will disappear.

On the other hand, if we speak and act strongly in one voice in defense of seed freedom, we can put the obscenity, violence, injustice, and immorality of patents on seeds and life behind us. In another era, slavery was made history. Just as today corporations see nothing wrong in owning life, slave owners saw nothing wrong in owning other humans. Just as people then questioned and challenged slavery, it is our ethical and ecological duty and right to challenge patents on seeds. We have a duty to liberate the seed and our farmers. We have a duty to defend our freedom and protect open source seeds as a commons. We have the duty and the right to defend life on Earth.

7

Localization Feeds the World,
Not Globalization

Two principles have shaped the evolution of food systems across the world. The first is that everyone must eat. The second is that every place where human beings live produces food. From the Arctic to the rainforest to the desert, each place has a different ecosystem, and hence a different food system, but there will be food wherever people are. Between these two principles, the food systems that have evolved to nourish people are, by their very nature, local. These systems of food production nourish both biological and cultural diversity. The localization of food is not only natural but vital, because it allows farmers to practice the Law of Return, produce more food through biodiversity, create food systems adapted to local cultures and ecologies, and nourish themselves, their communities, and the soil that they give back to.

Over the last twenty years, the globalization of food and agricultural systems has been presented as a natural and inevitable phenomenon. However, there is nothing natural about globalization, and in particular, the globalization of food.

The first wave of globalization began in the seventeenth century and was driven by Europe, which sought to control the spice trade from India. This is what led to the establishment of the East India Company and the signing of the first "free trade agreement" between the East India Company and the collapsing Mughal Empire. But the East India Company traded in spices, not staple foods. In fact, until the establishment of the World Trade Organization in 1995, food was a subject of local and national sovereignty, not of global trade.

The rules of global trade have been written by corporations in order to expand their control over food and agriculture, and thus increase their profits. The idea that free trade is based on competition is a myth. It has led to monopolies, with just five gene giants controlling seed—Monsanto, Syngenta, DuPont, Bayer, and Dow[1]—five grain giants controlling grain supply—Cargill, ADM (Archer Daniels Midland), Bunge, Glencore International, and Louis Dreyfus[2]—five processing giants controlling food and beverage processing—PepsiCo, JBS, Tyson Foods, Danone, and Nestlé[3]—and five retail giants controlling food retail—Walmart, Carrefour, Metro Group, Aeon, and Tesco.[4]

Just as false claims of feeding the world have been made about industrial agriculture as a model of production, false claims have been made about feeding the world through globalization, and free trade as a model of distribution. The reality is the opposite. Globalization has created displacement, unemployment, hunger, and food insecurity on an unprecedented scale. While the language used is "free trade" and competition, corporate globalization consists of unfair and unfree trade.

Globalization was imposed with the argument that it would do two things for food. First, that it would increase food production, under the theory that corporations are better at producing large amounts of things than small groups of people are. And second, that it would make food cheaper and therefore more accessible for the poor. Both these claims are lies. As far as food production goes, we've already seen how the "myth of more" produces less through monocultures, large farms, and poisons. In fact, globalization doesn't produce food; it produces commodities. Ninety percent of the corn and soy grown in the world is used for biofuel or animal feed, because that's where the largest profits lie. Commodities don't feed people; they create hunger.

As far as "cheap food" goes, globalized food is actually produced at a very high cost, and if it weren't for the fact that agribusinesses collect more than $400 billion in subsidies in rich countries, the entire system would collapse. Input costs—including fertilizers, pesticides, and machinery—are always higher than the value of what is traded, and without these subsidies, the system of globalized, mechanized food production would not work. These subsidized commodities are then in turn sold to poor countries, which are forced to dismantle their border protections so that rich nations can "dump" artificially cheap commodities into the developing world. To add to this, volatile global prices resulting from financial speculation further entrench a system that takes from farmers and people and gives to corporations and governments.

Globalization is implemented through neoliberal economic "reform" policies, which deregulate both domestic and international commerce, privatize public goods, and create a framework that accepts corporate rule.

Today, the world's food supply is in crisis. This crisis has multiple facets. First, the ecological costs of chemical-intensive, fossil-fuel-intensive industrial agriculture are massive, and are leading to climate change, biodiversity erosion, water depletion, and soil erosion. Second, globalized industrial agriculture is leading to the mass displacement of small-scale farmers, where on the one hand growing debt has pushed hundreds of thousands of farmers to suicide, and on the other hand, mass unemployment is feeding into different forms of extremism. Third, it is in the design of industrial food production to create hunger, malnutrition, and disease. Hunger is created by debt in situations where farmers are forced to sell what they grow; it is created by dumping, which destroys livelihoods; and it is created by turning food into a commodity for long-distance trade, which wastes large amounts of food.

Every dimension of the food crisis—nonsustainability, injustice, unemployment, hunger, and disease—is linked to the globalized, industrialized food system, and every dimension of the crisis can be addressed through ecological agriculture and local food systems. To grow sustainability, nutrition, and food democracy, we must think small, not big; local, not global.

Globalization benefits the wealthy (including wealthy countries) and exploits the poor. This is done in the name of "free trade," enacted through trade liberalization, or the dismantling of governmental restrictions on what and how much can be imported into a country. It is closely linked to the entrenchment of privatization, because when governments (are forced to) take a backseat through policies enforced by organizations such as the WTO, private companies step in and fill the gap. Trade liberalization is touted as an "opening up" of a country's borders to allow the easy flow of goods and services. In reality, the only stakeholders who benefit from these agreements are large private companies and rich nations. Over the last two decades, neoliberal policies have devastated livelihoods and food security across the world.

Trade liberalization forces poor countries to remove their import barriers, which leaves them vulnerable to "dumping," the process by which commodities that are subsidized in the Global North are "dumped" in large quantities into countries in the Global South. This creates the artificial impression that cheaper goods are now available in poorer countries. However, what this actually does is destroy local sources of food production and distribution, including farmers' livelihoods.

In 1998, when quantitative restrictions (or import barriers) were first dismantled in India, several commodities were dumped in order to undercut local food sources. Soy, at the time, was sold in the international market by the United States at $150 per metric ton. However, the subsidy (behind the production of soy) given to large farms and companies was $190 per metric ton. Without the subsidy, soy would have been unable to compete with local Indian produce. As this artificially cheap product flooded Indian markets, it began to undercut local farmers and local food production. This happened across crops. Where once the price of a coconut in Kerala was Rs. 10, after the dismantling of quantitative restrictions, it fell to Rs. 2 per nut. People in Kerala, the land of the coconut, began chopping down their trees and resorted to growing cash crops or selling their land.

One significant treaty that has allowed dumping to carry on at the expense of poorer countries is the Common Agricultural Policy (CAP) of the European Union, which is a system of agricultural subsidies. It was first implemented in 1962, but has since been revised several times to allow for larger-scale dumping into poor countries. In Jamaica, the dumping of heavily subsidized EU skim milk powder has led to a collapse in local dairy production. Ironically, EU dairy farmers have largely failed to benefit from the subsidies because payments are made directly to large food-processing companies rather than to the farmers themselves.[5]

In West Africa, between ten and eleven million farmers lost $200 million as a direct result of US subsidies, which are enacted through the US Farm Bill.[6] In South Africa, research shows that the European Union's sugar regime has enabled high-cost European farmers to benefit at the expense of much more efficient South African producers, resulting in lost jobs and revenue in a country battling both HIV/AIDS and the legacy of apartheid. Farmers in the Global South see CAP and the US Farm Bill as the worst examples of Northern double standards, summed up as "you liberalise, we subsidise."[7]

Due to the high levels of subsidies in the Global North, the removal of protective barriers transmits distorted price signals to domestic markets, which in turn pushes prices downward below survival levels. This also creates an imbalance in domestic supply and demand, and, as we will explore toward the end of the chapter, begins to aggressively reshape what food people can access.

The policies of trade liberalization go over and above dumping. These policies—touted as the pillars of liberalization—have undermined the government's role in ensuring food security for people and livelihood security for farmers. Advocates of trade liberalization call governmental measures meant to aid people "trade distorting" and demand that these be scrapped. In this way, when farmers and local producers are being put out of business by large quantities of imported goods, governments are unable to step in and help.

At the same time, rather than encourage community initiatives, trade liberalization has encouraged policies that give agribusiness increasing control over the food production and distribution system through programs such as "privatization," "market access," and the removal of quantitative restrictions on imports. An obvious example of the policy shift from people-centered concerns to trade- and corporation-centered concerns is the fact that farmers are not allowed by law to take their produce beyond state borders, whereas traders can pick up produce from anywhere and take it anywhere. In fact, governments (after forcibly taking away land from farmers and communities) are building superhighways to connect centers of agricultural production to airports and ports, so that corporations can quickly transport these commodities for export.

Whereas countries were once exporters, they have now become importers. In other words, they have moved from food-independent, self-sufficient economies to food-dependent economies. India, for example, has one of the largest vegetable oil economies in the world, and ranks first in the world's production of castor, safflower, sesame, and niger oil. In the span of a decade from 1985 to 1996, oilseed production more than doubled, and India achieved self-sufficiency. From 1990 to 1991, India exported Rs. 10,310 million of oilseeds. From 1991 to 1992, this went up to Rs. 16,500 million. However, with the introduction of trade liberalization and the dismantling of import barriers in 1998, India went from being a net exporter to a net importer of edible oils. By 2001, India was importing $133 million of edible oils; and by 2003, the import bill had jumped to $940.6 million, which accounts for 63.5 percent of our agri-imports.[8]

In 1992, Indonesian farmers produced enough soy to supply the entire domestic market. Soy-based tofu and tempeh are important parts of the daily diet across the archipelago. Following the implementation of a neoliberal doctrine, the country opened its borders to food imports, allowing cheap US soy (in other words, heavily subsidized US soy) to flood the market. This destroyed national production, and today 60 percent of the soy consumed in Indonesia is imported. Record prices for US soy in 2007 led to a national crisis in Indonesia, when the price of tempeh and tofu—known as the "meat of the poor"—doubled in just a few weeks.[9]

According to the FAO, the food deficit in West Africa increased by 81 percent between 1995 and 2004. During the same period, cereal imports increased by 102 percent, sugar imports by 83 percent, dairy products by 152 percent, and poultry by 500 percent. However, according to the International Fund for Agricultural Development (2007), the region has the potential to produce sufficient amounts of food. All across the world, liberalization goes on, even though it is increasing countries' vulnerabilities.[10]

The proponents of globalization depict trade liberalization as a policy intended to benefit all parties, and one that countries in the Global South have voluntarily signed up for. In reality, large companies and rich nations have put immense pressure on poorer countries to deregulate trade and open their markets to cheap imports.

The systems of industrial agriculture pushed by globalization pretend to be more efficient than organic small-scale farms by manipulating the definition of "yield" to include just one part of one crop. This is not real efficiency but only pseudoefficiency. In order to justify the industrial production of food and the policies of globalization and trade liberalization as the best framework in which to produce that food, pseudosurplus and pseudocompetition are added to the existing framework of pseudoefficiency.

The globalization of agriculture is the corporate control of agriculture. The 1995 WTO Agreement on Agriculture is an international treaty that forces countries to liberalize exports and imports, and allows global corporations to take control of domestic production, domestic markets, and global trade. The links between the treaty and the corporate sector are startlingly clear, since it was former Cargill Vice President Dan Amstutz who drafted its original text. The supply of grain across the world is almost entirely controlled by a handful of privately owned corporations: Cargill, Continental, ConAgra, Louis Dreyfus, Bunge, Garnac, Mitsui/Cook, and Archer Daniels Midland. Cargill recently bought Continental, making it the largest grain giant.

These grain giants are both the architects and the beneficiaries of the globalization of agriculture. They control agriculture and food production from seed to table and from farm to factory. They control the inputs farmers buy and the markets in which farmers sell their produce. Crucially, they determine the price at which farmers sell what they have grown. In the short run, they lower prices to capture markets. In the long run, such monopoly control leads to high food prices.

As farmers are forced to spend ever-increasing amounts on inputs while receiving less for their produce, food production has been transformed into a negative economy the world over. Low farm prices are usually explained as being the result of surpluses and overproduction. In reality, low prices are linked to monocultures and monopolies. When all farmers grow only one commodity, there will of course be a surplus of that one product. But this is a pseudosurplus, not a real surplus. It is not the surplus left after nature's needs for ecological maintenance have been met, or a farm family's needs for food and sustenance have been satisfied.

Industrial agriculture has meant that all the natural functions that biodiversity could perform for the farmer now have to be purchased. The same agribusiness corporations who sell external inputs to farmers also buy the farmers' produce. In India, where government support to farmers has been decreasing rapidly due to trade liberalization policies, the price of potatoes has fallen to Rs. 0.40 per kg. This allows large companies, such as PepsiCo and McDonald's, to pay farmers less than Rs. 0.08

to make potato chips they sell for Rs. 10 per 200 g. For thirteen million metric tons of potatoes, this amounts to a transfer of Rs. 20 billion from impoverished farmers and peasants to global multinational companies.[11] In Germany, farmers have seen the farmgate price of milk drop by 20–30 percent, pushing them into bankruptcy, because supermarkets use cheap dairy products as a marketing tool to attract consumers.

Low prices are not a result of higher production. In fact, prices are falling in spite of *lower* production, countering all commonly held supply and demand theories. Collapsing prices have more to do with the concentration of control than with excess supply. Farm prices are low because they are being "fixed" by corporate monopolies. Corporate giants can determine prices because farmers are locked into dependency for buying inputs and selling produce. For agribusiness, high production costs and low commodity prices translate into two-way profits. For the farmer, they translate into a negative economy and spiraling debt.

In this corporate-controlled system, the idea of "competition" is as false as the idea of "surplus." Neoliberal, "free market" policies suggest that a capitalist system of production encourages competition between companies and individuals, which results in the best and cheapest goods and services being made available to consumers. This is far from the truth. First, given that there are only a few companies who control nearly all the world's globalized food production, the competition is between agribusinesses that are more than happy to scratch each other's backs at the expense of small-scale farmers and common people.

Second, the very measure of "competitiveness" in the global free trade calculus is both fictitious and abstract, where the calculation is based on a comparison between the international price and the domestic price of a commodity. A paper from the Indian Ministry of Agriculture reads:

India is hard pressed to remove Quantitative Restrictions on imports.... In view of this, it is urgently needed that Indian farmers prepare themselves to face international competition.... Results based on the analysis of export competitiveness reveal that crops like rice, banana, grapes, sapota, lychees, onions, tomatoes and mushrooms are highly competitive. Crops like wheat, mangoes and potatoes are moderately competitive. The vulnerable section comprising less competitive or not competitive crops includes maize, sorghum, soybean, oil palm, pulses, coconut, clove, spices, jute and several other crops.[12]

The problem with competitiveness here is that it completely fails to take into account climate, ecology, local economies, and people's needs. When international prices are controlled by two or three corporations that also control the market for external inputs, prices can be fixed at extremely low levels. Governments in the Global North give massive subsidies to industrial farms and exporters, and just enough support to farmers to allow them to survive in negative agricultural economies. Then when these heavily subsidized commodities are dumped into the Global South, it is termed "competitiveness." Farmers in poorer countries who are producing food that people actually eat are then seen as unable to keep up with the "competition," and the destruction of farmers' livelihoods is presented by the proponents of globalization as inevitable.

Prices are not only artificially lowered, but also artificially raised. In many countries, large supermarkets have gained a near-monopoly power and are increasing prices far more than is justified by any actual price increase of the agricultural product. To add to this, international financial speculation has played a major role in food price increases since the summer of 2007. Due to the financial collapse in the United States, speculators moved from financial products to raw materials, which included agricultural products. This directly affects prices in domestic markets, because as we have seen, many countries are becoming increasingly dependent on food imports. Speculators bet on expected scarcity, even while production levels remain high. Based on these predictions, TNCs (transnational companies) have been manipulating the markets. Traders keep food stocks away from the market in order to stimulate price increases and generate huge profits afterward. In Indonesia, in the midst of the soy price hike in January 2008, the company PT. Cargill

Indonesia was still keeping 13,000 metric tons of soybeans in its ware-house in Surabaya, waiting for prices to reach record highs. This artificial inflation of prices is a result of the large sums of money to be made from financial speculation, and it creates hunger when there is actually enough food to feed everyone on the planet. As Kaufman writes, "Imaginary wheat bought anywhere affects real wheat bought everywhere."[13]

Unlike speculators and large traders, most peasants and farmers do not benefit from higher prices. If food comes from domestic producers, companies and other intermediaries that buy products from farmers and sell them at higher prices reap the benefits. If products come from the international market, it's even clearer who the beneficiaries are: transnational companies that control that market. These TNCs define what prices products are bought at in the country of origin and what prices products are sold at in the country of import. So even when prices do go up for producers, the biggest part of the increase is cashed in by others. In sectors with increasing production costs, such as dairy and meat, farmers even see their prices going down while prices for the consumer are shooting up. This is because, as we have seen, farmers sell their produce at an extremely low price compared to what consumers pay. In Europe, the Spanish Coordinator of Organizations of Farmers and Ranchers (COAG) calculated that consumers in Spain pay up to 600 percent more than what the food producer gets for his or her production. Similar figures also exist for other countries where the consumer price is defined mainly by costs for processing, transportation, and retailing.

Farmers, landless laborers, and consumers have all been hit hard by the crisis in food prices and food security. Agricultural workers as well as many people in rural areas now have to buy food, as they do not have access to land to produce their own. Some peasants and small-scale farmers may have land, but are forced to produce cash crops instead of food. These cash crops are less than profitable. For example, the increase of the price of edible oils in Indonesia since 2007 has not benefited the Indonesian palm oil farmers at all. Many of them are working under contract farming agreements with big agribusiness companies that process, refine, and sell the product. These companies increased domestic prices following the international price hike, but farmers themselves received only a minor price increase. The contract farming model creates a situation in which farmers cannot produce food for their families. Instead, they are forced to produce cash crops in monocultures such as sugarcane, palm oil, coffee, tea, and cacao. This means that even if the farmer receives a minor increase for her cash crop, she has to buy much more expensive food from the market to feed her family. In this way, increasing prices actually cause more poverty in farming families.

The international policies of the last few decades have expelled hundreds of millions of people from farms to urban centers, where most live in slums and eke out precarious livings. These urban dwellers are forced to work for very low wages and buy food and other goods at exorbitantly high prices. They are the first victims of the current crisis, since they have no way to produce their own food. Their number has increased dramatically, and they spend a big part of their income on food. According to the FAO, food represents up to 60–80 percent of consumer spending in developing countries (including landless farmers and agricultural workers).[14]

Even in rich countries of the Global North, hunger has emerged as an emergency. In the United States, 14.5 percent of households struggle to put enough food on the table. More than 48 million Americans, including 15.9 million children, are hungry.[15] In Britain, hunger is becoming a "public health emergency," according to a letter from scientists and doctors to the *British Medical Journal.* The number of cases of malnutrition has soared since the economic crisis began. In 2008, 3,161 patients were admitted to hospitals in the United Kingdom for malnutrition-related diseases; in 2012, the number rose to more than 5,000. In 2006, food banks fed 26,000 people; in 2012, the number exceeded 347,000.[16]

Through the removal of trade barriers and through the practice of dumping, governments are forced to import expensive food to meet consumer demand and do not have the means to support the poorest consumers. Companies ruthlessly exploit the current situation, accepting that the trade-off for profiteering is that increasing numbers of people go hungry.

Examples from countries across the world illustrate how policies of trade liberalization, dumping, and artificially inflated or reduced prices have destroyed food security. Here, we will look at two case studies.

KENYA

Like many African countries in the decades after colonial rule, Kenya received large amounts of aid in the form of loans to stabilize its economy. In 1980, in return for the aid it was unable to repay, Kenya was forced to liberalize its markets through a Structural Adjustment Loan from the World Bank. Under this new policy, the Kenyan government reduced support to its farmers, cut tariffs on imports, and deregulated its markets. In the early 1990s, Kenya joined the WTO, which allowed these policies to be more aggressively pursued. Cheap subsidized goods, from clothes to shoes to sugar to steel, flooded the country's markets. Thrown into competition with other countries, Kenya's fledgling industries and vulnerable farmers didn't stand a chance. Worse, the government was prevented from stepping in to help as a result of the agreements it had signed with the international community.[17]

The situation in Kenya has steadily worsened, and one of the most obvious impacts has been on food production and consumption. For example, the dairy industry was decimated due to cheaply available powdered milk, and the sugar industry was replaced by an influx of cheaper sugar. Like other postliberalization countries, Kenya also became an exporter of food. Each night, Kenya exports 350 metric tons of cut flowers and vegetables to be sold the next day in the United Kingdom. The largest percentage of exports to the United Kingdom are leguminous vegetables, which include peas, beans, and snow peas. In 2008, 1.3 million people in rural areas and nearly 4 million people in urban areas of Kenya were food insecure: they were hungry.[18] The World Food Programme says that Kenya has a yearly need of $300 million in food aid, whereas exporters say that Kenya exported more than $3 billion in food products in 2010. The companies exporting the food are large, multinational companies not owned by Kenyans.[19]

Trade liberalization in Kenya has not only destroyed local industries, but worsened people's standard of living. Changes in land ownership—from a commonly owned land system to one in which land is now registered under the male head of a family—have not only affected the types of food grown through a mass movement toward cash crops, but have pushed out the Masai, Kenya's nomadic tribal communities. Women, who make up the majority of food producers in the country, have borne the brunt of these changes. Men moved into new industries, leaving women with more responsibility for producing food, but with less freedom and space to decide what was being grown: because land is always in the man's name. Often, women are forced to shift to less nutritious crops that require less labor, or to rely on child labor, particularly girls.

Unemployment, poverty, and hunger have created several nexuses of violence and crime. Young adults, who are often poor and uneducated, are recruited by crime bosses in Somalia and Kenya to extort money from commercial and private ships in the Indian Ocean. There has also been an increase in trafficking in humans, weapons, and drugs. A 2001 survey found that between 90 and 95 percent of households in northern Kenya were armed.[20]

These are not accidental or inevitable situations, but a direct consequence of the policies of trade liberalization and globalization enforced since the late 1980s. Consider these figures. Data from 2005 shows that 56 percent of Kenyans live in poverty; in 1990, the figure was 48 percent. Data from 2005 shows that less than 30 percent of Kenyans are in formal employment; in 1988, the number was 70 percent. Data from 2005 shows that 48 percent of children in Kenya are not vaccinated; in 1993, the number was considerably less, at 31 percent.[21] As a consequence of liberalization, Kenya has an uneducated generation of young people, mass unemployment, and shattered industries that were once self-sustaining. Destroying a country's food security is the first and final step to destroying a country's well-being, and as a government paper read in 2003, "During the past two decades we have seen Kenya slide systematically into the abyss of underdevelopment and hopelessness."[22]

MEXICO

January 2014 marked the twenty-year anniversary of the day the Mexican government signed the North American Free Trade Agreement (NAFTA) together with the United States and Canada. Touted by then US president Bill Clinton as an attempt to close the wage gap between US and Mexican workers, the thrust of this 1994 "free trade" treaty was to remove tariffs on products being imported from the United States into Mexico. The last twenty years have shown NAFTA to be a key criminal in the systematic destruction of the Mexican people's standard of living, wealth, livelihoods, and economies; however, it is still claimed by the champions of liberalization to be a success. The only successes, however, have been for US or multinational corporations, and have been won at the expense of Mexico's people.

For more than ten thousand years, Mexican farmers have grown more than 209 varieties of maize, or corn. Approximately three million farmers grow maize, two-thirds of whom grow only just enough to feed their families.[23] Maize has always been the backbone of the Mexican diet. But today, these farmers are in crisis. The most drastic measure taken under NAFTA was the liberalization of the maize sector, which was dually implemented by expanding import quotas and reducing tariffs. Cheap maize from the United States—subsidized massively by the US government—flooded Mexican markets. During the first year of NAFTA, the price of maize in Mexico dropped by 20 percent, and carried on steadily declining throughout the 1990s.[24] Unable to compete with these falling prices, Mexican farming families have been forced to eke out dangerous, unsustainable, or violent livelihoods.

After NAFTA went into effect, many small-scale farmers were forced to take loans from drug mafias. Unable to repay their debts by selling the corn from their fields, farmers started to grow illicit drugs for the cartels. Today, Mexico is the largest supplier of marijuana and the third-largest supplier of heroin in the world. Most drug consumption takes place in rich countries, whereas most of its production takes place in—and at the expense of—poorer nations. Between 2007 and 2010 there were more than fifty thousand drug-related killings in Mexico.[25] Fields in which locally produced and nutritious food was once grown are today planted with poppies and marijuana, and fraught with violence and exploitation.

Having been forced out of farming, Mexicans have entered employment designed to prop up global companies. Areas of land are allocated to multinational companies to set up round-the-clock factories known as *maquiladoras,* where goods are manufactured or assembled for import. Existing in tax-free zones, these factories run unregulated and unchecked for twenty-four hours a day. After NAFTA was implemented, *maquiladoras* grew in number by 86 percent, and as of 2007, 1.3 million Mexicans were working in these factories.[26]

The movement toward a food-dependent economy has devastated various facets of Mexican people's lives. A system of collective land ownership, known as the *ejido* system, has been replaced with a system in which large portions of land can be sold off to companies and retailers. There has been a movement toward an illegal, violent economy after farming systems were interrupted. The safety of women, especially, has been lost—through both trafficking as well as a culture of violence resulting from indifferent, globalization-led policies and growth. The last two decades in Mexico have revealed the myth of "free trade," showing it to be a system of exploitation designed to only benefit those already in power.

Today, one billion people on the planet are hungry.[27] Paradoxically, half the hungry people in the world are growers of food. This is because globalization has enabled massive landgrabs, displaced farmers, and added millions to the ranks of the landless. The 2010 report of the UN Special Rapporteur on the Right to Food shows that more than five hundred million people dependent on small-scale agriculture are hungry, because they are unable to "compete" in global markets, and because their small plots of land are relegated to soils that are arid, hilly, or without irrigation. The more fertile lands have been bought up by agribusiness.[28] Globalization has led to a shift from "food first" to "export first" policies, in which growing luxury crops for export takes precedence over growing food crops for people. As chemical-intensive farming pushes more farmers to sell what they produce, it is evident that the debt trap is also a hunger trap.

In India, the capital of hunger, 214 million people are hungry. In sub-Saharan Africa, 198 million people are hungry; in China, 135 million are hungry; in other Asian and Pacific countries, 156 million are hungry; and in Latin America and the Caribbean, 56 million people are hungry.[29]

A global food crisis occurred in 2008, with food prices rising to unprecedented levels. According to the World Bank, rising food prices have caused fifty-one food riots in thirty-seven countries since 2007. A World Bank blog entry by Senior Economist José Cuesta entitled "No Food, No Peace" warns that "It is quite likely that we will experience more food riots in the foreseeable future ... food price shocks have repeatedly led to spontaneous—typically urban—sociopolitical instability."[30]

Just between 2005 and 2008, the international price of various foods increased by nearly half. While a metric ton of wheat was $152 in 2005, it went up to $343 in 2008; while rice was $207, it went up to $580; and while soy oil was $545, it escalated to $1,423.[31] In the face of these rising prices, then US President Bush used a fallacious argument to explain unaffordable food: he blamed the growing middle classes in developing countries. At a Missouri press conference on the economy, he said, "There are 350 million people in India who are classified as middle class. That's bigger than America. Their middle class is larger than our entire population. And when you start getting wealth, you start demanding better nutrition and better food so demand is high and that causes the price to go up."[32] This argument served both to divert US political debate away from the role of US agribusiness in precipitating the food crisis, and also to present economic globalization as benefiting countries like India.

But as the data shows, India is the hunger capital of the world, and as globalization becomes further entrenched, so does hunger. The myth that President Bush was propagating is a growth myth. It is being repeatedly stated that the price increase is due to "surging demand in emerging economies like China and India."[33] The argument is that since the economies of China and India have grown, the Chinese and the Indians have gotten richer and are eating more, and this increased demand is leading to higher prices. This growth myth is false on many counts. While the Indian economy has indeed grown, the majority of Indians have grown poorer, since as a direct result of globalization, they have lost both their land and their livelihoods. Most Indians are in fact eating less than before the era of globalization and trade liberalization.[34] The availability of food per capita has declined from 177 kg per person per year in 1991 to 152 kg per person per year in 2003. The daily availability of food has declined from 485 to 419 g/day, and the daily calorie intake has dropped from 2,220 cals/day to 2,150 cals/day. One million Indian children die every year from a lack of food.

The fact that India is the capital of hunger shows that growth does not reduce hunger, and the fact that most of the world's hungry people are themselves producers of food shows that the model of industrial agriculture is deeply implicated in the creation of hunger. Agricultural policies that push the small-scale farmer to destitution on the one hand and promote cash cropping on the other have resulted in lowered food production. There has been a steady decline in food production since the early 1990s as a result of the thrust toward export-oriented agriculture. The collapse of domestic support for food production (through dismantling import barriers, the rising costs of inputs, and crop failure due to uncertified seeds) in the late 1990s has intensified this shift from self-sustainable, food-independent populations to hungry, food-dependent ones.

Just as industrial production and globalized distribution reduce food to a commodity, the industrial processing of food reduces food to junk or to waste: it becomes antifood. As food becomes more synthetic, new health hazards are created, making food safety an increasing concern for citizens of the world.

As we have seen, globalization generates hunger and malnutrition. But the other side of this industrially processed food coin is obesity and other diet-related health conditions. In countries like the United States, the epidemic of obesity is highly visible, and it can be linked to food patterns in what investigative journalist Eric Schlosser has famously called a "Fast Food Nation." An Indiana University study finds that between 1976 and 1980, there was a sharp incline in the number of Americans who went from "overweight" to "obese." This increase, researchers find, is linked to not only the percentage of fat and sugar being consumed by Americans (USDA data shows that between 1970 and 2003, fat consumption in the United States increased by 63 percent and sugar consumption by 19 percent), but to the *types* of sugar and fat being consumed.

Take sugar. In the 1970s, technology was developed to turn corn-starch into glucose. This eventually became HFCS, or high fructose corn syrup. Aided by the government's subsidization of the corn industry, HFCS became the most cost-effective replacement for sugar.[35] As globalization, large-scale farming, and industrially processed food became the dominant means of food production in the United States, the consumption of HFCS increased more than 1,000 percent between 1970 and 1990. American Society for Clinical Nutrition data from 2004 demonstrates that due to the difference in digestion, absorption, and metabolism between sucrose (normal sugar) and fructose (which makes up HFCS), the increase in HFCS consumption can be temporally linked to the obesity epidemic in the United States.[36]

Obesity, contrary to popular views, is not the prerogative of rich, developed countries. Rather, the globalization of a handful of commodities has meant that poor nutrition is being exported worldwide, in what is often known as the McDonaldization of world food. Globally, PepsiCo had an annual revenue of $66.68 billion in 2014,[37] and holds the world's largest portfolio of billion-dollar food and beverage brands and several product lines, including Frito-Lay, Quaker, Pepsi-Cola, Tropicana, and Gatorade. PepsiCo describes these as "nourishing, tasty foods and drinks that bring joy to our consumers in more than 200 countries."[38]

PepsiCo entered India in 1989 during the Punjab crisis to replace rice and wheat with tomatoes and potatoes, supposedly to feed people. But rice and wheat can be stored, whereas tomatoes and potatoes are perishable commodities: they decrease food security and increase farmers' vulnerability to the market. In any case, the tomatoes grown by PepsiCo were bred for long-distance transportation and industrial processing, and the skin was too hard for domestic use in cooking. The potatoes were used for Lay's potato chips.

In 1994, PepsiCo was given permission to start sixty restaurants in India: thirty KFCs (Kentucky Fried Chickens) and thirty Pizza Huts. As early as 1977, the US Senate identified the processed meats and chicken available at these restaurants as a source of the cancers that one American contracts every seven seconds.[39] Since its entry into India, PepsiCo has destroyed millions of jobs by displacing local livelihoods and food sources, and today, 25 percent of schoolchildren in Delhi suffer from obesity as a result of the large quantities of cheap junk food now freely available throughout the country.[40]

India is also becoming the world capital for diabetes, projected to soon overtake China. Data from the International Diabetes Federation indicates that 65.1 million Indians suffer from diabetes today, whereas in 2008, the number was 50.8 million. Despite these alarming statistics, a recent report shows that the fast-food market is likely to double in the next three years.[41]

Ironically, while one in every four Indians goes hungry due to the displacement of local food sources and farmers' livelihoods, an urban upper class is suffering from diabetes and obesity, which stem from exactly the same source.

Climate change today is global in cause and global in effect: trade liberalization and corporate globalization are causing climate change in several ways. Most significantly, resource- and energy-intensive polluting industries are moving to countries in the Global South. In 1991 the World Bank's chief economist Lawrence Summers wrote a memo to senior World Bank staff in which he said, "Just between you and me, shouldn't the World Bank be encouraging more migration of the dirty industries to the LDCs [less developed countries]?"[42]

Summers justified the economic logic of increasing pollution in the Global South on three grounds. First, since wages are low in the Global South, the economic costs of pollution arising from increased illness and death are lowest in the poorest countries. Second, since many countries in the Global South still have low pollution rates, according to Summers it makes economic sense to introduce pollution. And third, he argues that since the poor are poor, they cannot possibly worry about environmental problems.

Today, this mercenary logic is being put into practice, and in India, for example, we are seeing an explosion of steel, aluminum, and sponge iron production; automobile manufacture; and petrochemical industries, all of which lead to increased CO_2 emissions.

As local economies and production are destroyed, more carbon dioxide is being added to the atmosphere to meet the same human needs. This is because the production, transportation, refrigeration, and packaging of global food commodities require more fossil fuels. We are also seeing the destruction of local economies and local production, and as a result, more carbon dioxide is being added to the atmosphere to meet the same human needs. Through these processes, the burden of global industrial production is now falling on poorer countries, and, in a distorted paradigm, the pollution caused by these industries is being presented as proof of development.

Another way in which globalization is causing climate change is through food miles. Food miles are the distance food travels from where it is produced to where it is consumed. A study by the Danish Ministry of the Environment showed that 1 kg of food moving across the world generates 10 kg of carbon dioxide.[43] A study in Canada calculated that in 2003, food in Toronto traveled an average of 3,333 miles.[44] In the United Kingdom, the distance traveled by food increased by 50 percent between 1978 and 1999.[45] And alarmingly, a Swedish study found that the food miles of a typical morning breakfast are a distance equivalent to the circumference of the Earth.[46]

Very often, all that globalization achieves is a food swap, which again contributes to food miles. Tracy Worcester writes in *Resurgence:*

> In 1996, Britain exported 111 million litres of milk and imported 173 million litres. It imported 49 million kilograms of butter but it exported 47 million. Why didn't it just consume its own 47 million kilos and import the shortfall of 2 million, thus saving all the transportation costs? Why? Because not importing and exporting on a grand scale produces no profits for the transnational and their transport leets. The food giants will fly apples to Britain from 14,000 miles away in New Zealand and bring green beans 4,000 miles from Kenya, although British farmers can easily grow both.[47]

Globalization leads to waste at multiple levels, and the FAO estimates that 30 percent of the global food supply is wasted, totaling $1 trillion of food waste each year. Data shows that half the industrialized world's food is wasted by retailers or consumers, while there are growing losses after harvest in the Global South.

Long-distance food chains destroy food at both the level of production and the level of distribution. Wastage begins with how food is grown. Industrial agriculture is based on monocultures and the destruction of biodiversity: this biodiversity is food. But a centralized and globalized supply of food promotes uniformity. The apple and peach must be the exact shape and size demanded by the retailer, and the cabbage and lettuce must be uniform before they can be "counted." This leads to massive waste at the farm level.

Safe food is a vital component of food security. However, pseudosafety standards being imposed in the name of "modernization" do not guarantee safe food. Uniformity in the shape and size of fruits and vegetables has nothing to do with safety. Using the standards of industrial food processing to shut down artisanal production and local processing is a forced replacement of healthy, safe, culturally diverse food with unhealthy, processed junk food. It is a *waste* of real food that real people eat.

The FAO's Food Wastage Footprint project shows that in addition to the retail cost of food, another $700 billion is wasted in natural resources, including $172 billion in wasted water, $42 billion in cleared forest, and $429 billion in greenhouse gas costs. Such ecological destruction of natural capital is justified in terms of "feeding people."[48]

It is a *waste* to use food to drive cars. It is a *waste* to use 10 kg of food grain to produce 1 kg of meat. A food system that focuses on profits, rather than the health and well-being of people or the planet, will waste not only food, but also people and the planet. Indeed, half of India's children are so severely malnourished that they are technically described as *wasted*. And, according to the FAO, the 70 percent of food not wasted but doused in pesticides costs us $350 billion in health treatment every year: a *waste* of money.[49]

Subsidies worth $400 billion each year are wasted to keep this system artificially afloat. "Cheap" commodities have very high financial, ecological, and social costs. Industrial chemical agriculture displaces productive rural families. It creates debts, which, alongside mortgages, are the main reason for the disappearance of the family farm. In extreme cases, as in the cotton belt of India, such debt has pushed more than 284,000 farmers to suicide since 1995.[50] These are *wasted* lives.

"Freedom" has become such a contested term. When I say "freedom," I use it to refer to people's freedom to live freely, have livelihoods, and access vital resources, including seed, food, water, and land. I use "freedom" to talk about the freedom of the Earth and all her beings.

But corporations also use the word "freedom." "Free trade" rules are written by corporations to enlarge their freedom to commodify and privatize the last inch of land, the last drop of water, the last seed, and the last morsel of food. In the process, they destroy the freedom of the Earth and the Earth Family, and destroy the freedom of people to enjoy their livelihoods, cultures, and democracies.

We want freedoms for people, not corporations. We want governments to regulate corporations that cause harm, not police citizens through undemocratic seed laws and food laws whose only objective is to criminalize citizen freedoms in order to establish corporate totalitarianism over our seed and food. These freedoms can be attained only when we move from big to small, from global to local.

Navdanya's research and practice show that an ecological approach to agriculture through localized and decentralized food systems delivers higher benefits in terms of food security and food sovereignty than industrial agriculture. Diversity goes hand in hand with decentralization, and the creation of decentralized, biodiverse food systems is the key to the design of a world without hunger. For this, a shift from globalization to localization is vital. Globalization has reduced food to a commodity while expanding the control of agribusiness. Localization reclaims food as nourishment, expands community control over food systems, and promotes food democracy and food sovereignty.

In a globalized system, agriculture and food systems are shaped and controlled by corporations; in a localized system, they are shaped and controlled by communities. Whereas globalization is based on chemicals and GMOs that bring profits to corporations, localization is based on biodiversity and agroecology, which bring benefits to ecosystems and communities. Globalized agriculture views seeds as the intellectual property of corporations; localized agriculture views seeds as the common property of communities. Globalization creates monocultures of a few commodities; localization nourishes the biodiversity of plants, animals, and ecosystems. Food under globalization is a commodity; food under localization is a source of nourishment and a human right. In a globalized system, commodity speculation drives prices; in a localized system, prices are fixed by principles of justice and fairness. A globalized system of food has led to one billion hungry people, and another two billion suffering from food-related diseases; a localized food system, on the other hand, will see the end of hunger and malnutrition, and provide good food for all people. Finally, globalization runs on a system of food dictatorship, whereas localization functions according to a system of food sovereignty and food democracy.

We urgently need to design a transition from a globalization paradigm to a localization paradigm. This does not mean an end to international trade. But it does mean prioritizing the local. It means the decommodification of food to reclaim food as our being, our nourishment, our identity, and our human right. It means getting agriculture out of WTO rules and governing it on the principles of food sovereignty. It means getting gamblers away from our food before they bring down the food economy like they brought down the financial economy. It means stopping landgrabs and the diversion of food for the poor into fuel for the cars of the rich. It means remembering that everything is food, we are what we eat, and at the biological level, food justice is an ecological imperative. As biological beings, we all have an equal right to the Earth's resources and to their potential to provide food for all. Seedgrab, landgrab, and foodgrab violate the ethical and ecological design of what it means to be human. Hunger by design is immoral, unjust, and nonsustainable. We are capable of making a transition to a better design that is ethical, just, and sustainable.

How can we make this transition happen? First, countries should give priority in their budgets to support the poorest consumers so that they have access to sufficient food. Second, countries should give priority to their domestic food production in order to become less dependent on the world market. This means an increased investment in peasant- and farmer-based food production. We *do* need more intensive food production, but intensive in the use of labor and in the sustainable use of natural resources. Diverse production systems have to be developed to integrate local foods that have been neglected since the onset of the Green

Revolution. Small-scale family farms can produce a large diversity of food that guarantees both a balanced diet and some surpluses for the markets. Third, internal market prices have to be stabilized at a reasonable level for farmers and consumers—for farmers so that they can receive prices that cover the cost of production and secure a decent income, and for consumers so that they are protected against high food prices. Direct sales from peasants and small-scale farmers to consumers have to be encouraged.

Fourth, in every country an intervention system has to be put in place that can stabilize market prices. In order to achieve this, import controls with taxes and quotas are needed to regulate imports and avoid dumping or low-price imports that undermine domestic production. National buffer stocks of food managed by the state have to be built up in order to stabilize domestic markets; in times of surplus, cereals can be taken from the market to build up the cereal stock, and in case of shortage, cereals can be released.

Finally, to make this happen, land must be distributed equally to the landless and to peasant families through genuine agrarian reforms and land reforms. This should include control over and access to water, seed, credits, and appropriate technology. People should be enabled once again to produce their own food and feed their own communities. Any landgrabbing, land evictions, and expansions of land allocation for agribusiness-led agriculture have to be stopped.

Two decades of globalization have left us with an agrarian crisis, a food crisis, a disease epidemic, food waste, and a deepening of the ecological crisis. As a food system, industrial globalization has failed the planet and humanity. We now need to make a transition to systems of production and distribution of food that concentrate on local economies and local food systems. These localized systems bring us real and living food, which is part of the web of life. Here, food is produced by real farmers who work with living seed and living soil, not by global corporations. We need to break away from the rules of agriculture written by global corporations and write new rules: ones written by the people, for the people, through a real food democracy.

8

Women Feed the World, Not Corporations

Women, who are the primary growers and providers of food, nutrition, and nourishment in societies across the world, have evolved agriculture. Most farmers in the world are women, and most girls are future farmers: they learn the skills and knowledge of farming in fields and in farms. Women-centered food systems are based on sharing and caring, and on conservation and well-being. What is grown on farms determines whose livelihoods are secured, what is eaten, how much is eaten, and by whom it is eaten. Women's food is diverse and sustaining, and when women control the food system, everyone gets their fair share to eat. Women are the world's biodiversity experts, nutritional experts, and the economists who know how to produce more using less. Women make the most significant contributions to food security by producing more than half the world's food and by providing more than 80 percent of the food needs of food-insecure households and regions.[1]

But corporate globalization driven by a capitalist patriarchy has transformed food: what it contains, how it is produced, and how it is distributed. Corporate-controlled food is no longer food; it is a commodity manufactured for profit. Food—or what corporations call food—can be casually interchanged between biofuel for driving a car, feed for factory farms, and sustenance for the hungry. Today, just a handful of corporations control the global food system, and through this monopoly, food has been displaced and women's knowledge, work, skills, and creativity have been destroyed. The control over the entire food chain, from seed to table, is shifting from women's hands into the greedy hands of global corporations, who are today's global patriarchs.

Women have vast knowledge of seed, biodiversity, and nutrition. The knowledge that governs women's food is nonmechanistic, nonreductionist, and deeply rooted in the principles of agroecology. Women do more work than anyone else in growing and processing food, and their knowledge of farming is more sophisticated than industries and so-called "experts" promoting industrial agriculture. They are smarter at providing nutrition through biodiversity than the "miracles" being offered by biotechnologists through genetic engineering.

Yet neither women's knowledge nor their work is taken into account by the structures of patriarchal science and patriarchal economics. Patriarchal science is based on an artificial construction of a fictitious "creation boundary." This creation boundary erases the creativity and intelligence of nature and women, and renders their knowledge invisible. Patriarchal economics, in turn, renders women invisible as farmers through the creation of an unjust "production boundary," where the rules of GDP and official "jobs" mean that if you consume what you produce, you do not "count" as a producer. Patriarchal economics constructs a production boundary that excludes women's work, which is for sustenance, not profiteering at the cost of nature and people.

In agriculture—as in other sciences and areas of economic activity—women's scientific and economic contribution has been erased. Women's work in food and agriculture has been made invisible, even though it is the foundation of society. Sustainable food systems shaped by women for sustaining their families, communities, biodiversity, and the Earth are thus reduced to zero in this patriarchal productivity calculus and the patriarchal scientific calculus.

Corporations, on the other hand, exist only to make profit. As they enter the arenas of seed, food, and agriculture, they destroy the nourishing and sustaining qualities of the food system and transform everything into a commodity to be traded for profit. Women's knowledge and work are destroyed, and with it the health of the planet and its people is also devastated.

Industrial agriculture is rooted in a patriarchal scientific paradigm that privileges violence, fragmentation, and mechanistic thought. Rooted in ideologies of war, this paradigm promotes Monocultures of the Mind and monocultures on our land, denying the knowledge of agroecology and of diversity, which is women's knowledge. The implementation of this violent paradigm as the dominant lens for understanding our place in the world began with the "fathers of modern science": Bacon, Newton, and Descartes. As we saw in Chapter One, the Newtonian-Cartesian idea of nature as a fragmented world denies the interconnectedness of nature and has subsequently been proved false by new sciences such as quantum physics and epigenetics.

According to Bacon, the discipline of scientific knowledge and the mechanical inventions it leads to do not "merely exert a gentle guidance over nature's course; they have the power to conquer and subdue her, to shake her to her foundations."[2] In *The Masculine Birth of Time,* Bacon promised to create "a blessed race of heroes and supermen"[3] that would dominate both nature and society. The gendered violence of his words are unmistakable: heroes and super*men* will dominate and shake nature to *her* foundations.

The Royal Society, founded in 1660 in London, is seen as being instrumental in the Scientific Revolution of the seventeenth and eighteenth centuries. The society was inspired by Bacon's philosophy and seen by its organizers as a masculine project. In 1664 its secretary, Henry Oldenburg, announced that the intention of the society was to "raise a masculine philosophy. whereby the Mind of the Man may be ennobled with the knowledge of solid truths."[4] Joseph Glanvill, another fellow of the Royal Society, held that the masculine aim of science was to know "the ways of captivating Nature, and making her subserve our purposes, thereby achieving the Empire of Man Over Nature."[5]

Scientist Robert Boyle, a founding fellow of the Royal Society and governor of the New England Company, saw the rise of mechanical philosophy as an instrument of power: not just over nature, but also over the original inhabitants of America. He explicitly declared his intention of ridding the New England Indians of their "ridiculous" notions about the workings of nature. He attacked their perception of nature "as a kind of goddess" and argued that "the veneration, wherewith men are imbued for what they call nature, has been a discouraging impediment to the empire of man over the inferior creatures of God."[6]

The death of nature in the mind allows a war to be unleashed against the Earth. After all, if the Earth is merely dead matter, then nothing can be killed. As feminist historian Carolyn Merchant points out, this transformation of nature from a living, nurturing mother to inert, dead, and manipulable matter was eminently suited to the exploitation imperative of growing capitalism. The nurturing Earth image acted as a cultural constraint on the exploitation of nature, and as Merchant writes, "One does not readily slay a mother, dig into her entrails or mutilate her body."[7] But the images of mastery and domination created by the Baconian program and the masculine thrust of the Scientific Revolution removed all restraint, and functioned as cultural sanctions for the denudation of nature.

Feminine knowledge of agriculture has evolved over five thousand years. While the Scientific Revolution remained blind to this knowledge, it was unable to destroy the foundations of food and agriculture. But now, in less than two decades and with the rise of global corporations, genetic engineering, and patents, a direct assault on women's knowledge and production is taking place.

Global corporations have used the foundations laid by masculine science to render women's knowledge and productivity invisible by ignoring the dimension of diversity in agricultural production. As an FAO report entitled "Women Feed the World" mentions,[8] women use more plant diversity—both cultivated and uncultivated—than agricultural scientists know about. In Nigerian home gardens, women plant 18–57 plant species in a single home garden. In sub-Saharan Africa, women cultivate as many as 120 different plants in the spaces left alongside the cash crops managed by men. In Guatemala, home gardens that account for less than 0.1 hectare of land grow more than ten tree and crop species.

In a single African home garden, more than 60 species of food-producing trees were counted. In Indian agriculture, women use 150 different species of plants for vegetables, fodder, and health care. In West Bengal, 124 "weed" species collected from rice fields are shown to have economic and nutritional importance for farmers. In Veracruz, Mexico, peasants utilize approximately 435 wild plant and animal species, of which 229 are eaten. Women are the biodiversity experts of the world.[9] Unfortunately, girls are being denied their potential as food producers and as biodiversity experts under the dual pressures of invisibility and the domination of industrial agriculture.

While women manage and produce diversity, the dominant paradigm of agriculture promotes monocultures under the false tenet that monocultures produce more. But monocultures do not produce more; they simply concentrate control and power in the hands of a few corporations. The systemic erosion of women's knowledge of agriculture has violated women's position as experts in agriculture, and since their expertise is related to modeling agriculture on nature's methods of renewability, the destruction of this knowledge has gone hand in hand with the ecological destruction of nature's processes, and the destruction of people's livelihoods and lives.

Patriarchal economics constructs an imaginary production boundary that denies production that takes place in nature's economy and in people's sustenance economies. The exploitation of resources and people is then presented as production and growth. GDP is based on a false assumption: if you consume what you produce, you don't produce. Women's work in the food economy is thus reduced to zero, even though it is their work that keeps people fed.

This patriarchal economics has rendered women's work as food providers invisible because women provide for households not companies, and also because women perform multiple tasks involving diverse skills. Women have remained invisible as farmers in spite of their contribution to farming, because a patriarchal economic system fails to count women's production as "work," since it falls outside the production boundary. These problems with collecting data on agricultural work arise not because too few women work, but because too many women do too many different *kinds* of work. There is a conceptual inability of statisticians and researchers to define women's work both inside and outside the home, and farming is usually part of both. This lack of recognition of what is and is not labor is exacerbated both by the great volume of work that women do and the fact that they do many chores at the same time. It is also related to the fact that although women work to sustain their families and communities, most of their work is not measured in wages. Like all farmers, women do not have "jobs"; they have livelihoods.

Wages are paid in money, but money no longer signifies just a payment or a means of payment. Corporations have redefined the concept of money and turned it into "capital." In this process, the creativity of women's work has been erased. The Latin root of the word "capital" is *caput,* which means "the head." Money, the means used by real people to produce real wealth, is made to look as if corporations were producing it. Corporate exploiters then manipulate the meaning of "capital" to turn themselves into the "head": to rule over and exploit nature and people. Today, with the advent of globalization and TNCs, all the discourse about economics is reduced to "foreign investment," and like "capital," "investment" is a construct behind which the 1 percent hide to rob the 99 percent of their resources and opportunities.

In *Integral Economics,* Ronnie Lessem and Alexander Schieffer have reflected that

> If the fathers of capitalist theory had chosen a mother rather than a single bourgeois male as the smallest economic unit for their theoretical constructions, they would not have been able to formulate the axiom of the selfish nature of human beings in the way they did.[10]

Today, who or what counts as a human being is changing. Beginning with the idea of a bourgeois male as the normative "human," patriarchal economics constructed the "corporation" as a patriarchal person. Seed, food, and agriculture, which are women's spheres of knowledge and production, are simultaneously ignored in the dominant economy while also being seen as sources of mega profits for corporations.

The first corporations, like the British East India Company, were established during colonial rule as "limited liability companies," with associations of rich European men forming companies to privatize profits and socialize losses. Over time, especially in the United States, corporations started to be treated as natural persons instead of artificial legal constructs. In fact, the Fourteenth Amendment, which was added to the US Constitution to protect the rights of freed slaves, was reinterpreted so as to cover corporations.[11]

With the rights of natural persons, corporations could now begin undermining the rights of real people. They could start blocking democratically institutionalized laws to protect citizens by claiming that their Fourteenth Amendment freedoms were being interfered with. Today, corporations are claiming that their economic power to influence elections, to control seeds, and to dominate our food system is a part of their "freedom of speech." In May 2014, the state of Vermont passed the first GMO labeling law in the United States. In response, Monsanto, together with the largest junk-food lobby in the country—the Grocery

Manufacturers Association (GMA)—claimed that this "impose[d] burdensome new speech requirements."[12] In this way, the right to *hide* information about poisons was portrayed by Monsanto as the right to free speech. Today, sixty countries across the world have mandatory GMO labeling laws, but several efforts in other US states to pass these laws have been blocked by industry. In California and Washington, Monsanto and the GMA spent nearly $100 million to defeat the vote in favor of labeling.

When artificial entities like corporations are treated as natural persons, their rights become absolute and they can undermine the rights of all species, all people, and all women. A corporation does not have a mind of its own, but now it can appropriate people's collective wealth of seed and seed knowledge that women have conserved over millennia through intellectual property rights. A corporation produces nothing, but through free trade rules it can now appropriate all the food in the world produced by farmers and turn it into a commodity. A corporation cannot vote, but it can steal elections through corporate funding. Limits on financing elections were interpreted by the US Supreme Court as interferences with the "free speech" of a corporation.[13]

The control of corporations over the food system is not just leading to the marginalization of women's knowledge and productive capacity, but it is also undermining the potential of our species to feed itself. Five gene giants and five food giants have replaced billions of women producers and processors, which has created global food insecurity. More than one billion people are denied access to food, and another two billion are cursed with obesity and related diseases due to industrially processed junk food. Among those who suffer the two kinds of malnutrition, women and girls are the worst sufferers. This is why half the world's hungry population are food growers: most of them are women.

A scientific and economic model based on violence toward the Earth is directly linked to real violence against women. When I was studying the Green Revolution in Punjab, I saw the first advertisements for sex-selective abortion handpainted on walls. A model of agriculture that had displaced women from their productive work in agriculture by replacing them with chemicals and machines was now making them a disposable sex. Based on the declining sex ratio across the world (a figure that measures the number of women per thousand men), economist Amartya Sen has said that more than one hundred million women are missing.[14] As a masculine model of production systemically devalues women's place in the world, women themselves are devalued, displaced, and disappeared. The growing incidence and brutality of rapes worldwide is also related to a violent economy that transforms every being into a commodity, including and especially women. And as millions are uprooted and displaced, brutalized men brutalize women.

Seed is the first link in the food chain. For five thousand years, peasants have produced their own seeds, selecting, storing, replanting, and letting nature take its course in the food chain. Feminine principles have governed the conservation of seeds, and through seed conservation, women preserve genetic diversity and the self-renewability of food crops. This sustainable knowledge and agricultural practice that is the foundation for the emerging paradigm of agroecology was ruptured by the Green Revolution.

At the heart of the Green Revolution lay new varieties of "miracle" seeds, which have entirely transformed the nature of food production. The "miracle" seeds for which Borlaug received a Nobel Prize and that rapidly spread across the third world also sowed the seeds of a new commercialization of agriculture. Borlaug ushered in an era of corporate control of food production by creating a technology through which multinationals acquired control over seeds and hence over the entire food system. The Green Revolution commercialized and privatized seeds, removing control of plant genetic resources from peasant women in the Global South. This control was in turn given to male technocrats in international research centers run by the World Bank—such as the CIMMYT and IRRI—and to multinational corporations.

Women have acted as the custodians of genetic heritage for centuries. In a study of rural women in Nepal, it was found that seed selection is primarily a female responsibility. In 60.4 percent of the examples in the study, women alone decided what type of seed to use, while men decided in only 20.7 percent of the examples. In cases where families use their own seeds, the decision is made by women alone 81.2 percent of the time.[15] Women have carefully maintained the genetic base of food production for thousands of years. But now, a masculine viewpoint of seeds defines this common wealth as "primitive," and sees its own new products as "advanced" varieties.

The Green Revolution was a strategy based on breeding out the feminine principle by destroying the self-reproducing characteristic and genetic diversity of seeds. The death of the feminine principle in plant breeding was the beginning of seeds becoming a source of profits and control. But the hybrid "miracle" seeds are a commercial miracle because farmers have to buy new supplies of them every year; they do not reproduce themselves. Hybrids do not produce seeds that duplicate the same result because hybrids do not pass on their vigor to the next generation. With hybridization, seeds are no longer a source of plant life, producing sustenance through food and nutrition; they are now a source of private profit.

Green Revolution seeds did not increase food production from the point of view of nature, women, and poor peasants. These varieties were useful only for corporations that wanted to find new avenues of profit in seed and fertilizer sales. The international agencies that financed research on the new seeds also provided the money for their distribution. The impossible task of selling a new variety to millions of small peasants who could not afford to buy these seeds was solved by the World Bank, the United Nations Development Programme, the FAO, and a host of bilateral aid programs, which began to accord high priority to the distribution of HYV seeds. The Green Revolution has spread monocultures of chemical rice and wheat through both hybrid seeds and GMOs, driving out biodiversity, and hence nutrition, from our farms and diets.

Those crops that survived this chemical onslaught, such as spontaneous crops like the amaranth greens and chenopodium (*bathua*)—which are rich in iron—were then sprayed with poisons and herbicides. Instead of being seen as iron-rich and vitamin-rich gifts, these crops are treated as "weeds." A Monsanto representative once said that genetically engineered crops resistant to their proprietary herbicide Roundup killed the weeds that "steal the sunshine." And Monsanto's ads for Roundup in India tell women, "Liberate yourself, use Roundup." But GMOs are a recipe for neither women's liberation nor food liberation, but for malnutrition.

Instead of growing biodiversity and following the Law of Return to give nutrients back to the soil so that food is full of nutrients, and instead of growing food democracy to ensure everyone in society has access to healthy, safe, and nutritious food, capitalist patriarchy turns the malnutrition crisis it has created through Monocultures of the Mind and mechanistic science into its next market opportunity.

After the failure of Bt and HT crops to increase yields, decrease chemical use, or control weeds and pests, biofortification through genetic engineering has become the next big push of global agribusinesses. Two such initiatives in India were the introduction of golden rice to remove vitamin A deficiency and supposedly end blindness, and iron-enriched GMO bananas, to prevent Indian women from dying in childbirth because of iron-deficiency anemia.

But in reality, golden rice is far less efficient than available alternatives, and the promoters of golden rice themselves admit that it produces only 35 micrograms (µg) per gram of rice.[16] Biodiversity and ecological agriculture offer us alternatives that are 350–600 percent richer in vitamin A than golden rice. Some of these alternatives that are commonly used in Indian food include amaranth leaves, which have 14,190 µg of vitamin A per 100 g; drumstick leaves at 19,690 µg; spinach at 5,580 µg; and carrots at 6,460 µg of vitamin A per 100 g. In contrast, only 3,500 µg of vitamin A are found in every 100 g of golden rice. The knowledge of these alternatives has always been in women's hands, farmlands, and control. Today, this knowledge and practice are being displaced by a biofortification that will actually *decrease* vitamin A availability and create profits for ever-growing corporations.[17]

Iron-rich bananas are just as much of a myth. The same scientist—James Dale from Queensland University of Technology, Australia—who is beginning human trials of vitamin A-rich bananas in Uganda is claiming to end mothers' deaths after childbirth by fortifying bananas with iron, to prevent iron-deficiency anemia. After a decade of research and development, the GMO iron-rich banana will provide 2–3 mg of iron in 100 g of food. This is vastly inferior to what women's knowledge offers. For example, amaranth has 11 mg of iron per 100 g of food, neem has 25.3, rice bran has 35, lotus stems have 60, and mango powder has 45.2 mg of iron per 100 g of food. These are only a few of countless indigenous sources of iron found in the Indian diet. In fact, because iron absorption increases with vitamin C, women's knowledge has ensured that vitamin C-rich chutneys are eaten as a part of the diet. This knowledge is being discounted and erased.[18]

The solution to malnutrition lies in growing nutrition, and growing nutrition means growing biodiversity. It means recognizing the knowledge of biodiversity and nutrition among millions of Indian women who have received it for generations as grandmothers' knowledge. But there is a creation myth that is blind to nature's creativity and biodiversity, and to the creativity, intelligence, and knowledge of women. According to this creation myth of patriarchal science, rich and powerful men are the "creators." They can own life through patents and intellectual property. They can tinker with nature's complex evolution over millennia and claim that their trivial yet destructive acts of gene manipulation "create" life, "create" food, and "create" nutrition.

GMOs for biofortification are part of a patriarchal project that renders invisible and displaces women's superior knowledge of biodiversity and nutrition. In the case of GM bananas, it is *one* rich man—Bill Gates—financing *one* Australian scientist—Dale—who knows *one* crop—the banana—to then impose inefficient and hazardous GM bananas on millions of people in India and Uganda, who have grown hundreds of banana varieties for thousands of years, in addition to thousands of other crops.

The answer to malnutrition does not lie in monocultures and a masculine corporate domination of our seeds and food. It lies in the biodiversity in our farms and gardens, and in the cultural diversity of our food systems: it lies in women's hands and in women's minds.

Agricultural systems shaped by women have a number of key features: farming is done on a small scale, natural resources are conserved and renewed, and there is little or no dependence on fossil fuels and chemicals.

Inputs needed for production, such as fertilizers, are produced on the farm from compost, green manures, or nitrogen-fixing crops. Diversity and integration are key features, and nutrition is a key consideration. Women who run small farms maximize nutrition per acre and health per acre, while they conserve resources.

With food grown for eating, most food is consumed at the household or local level, some is marketed locally, and only some goes to distant places. Women-centered agriculture is the basis of food security for rural communities. When the household and the community are food secure, female children are food secure. When the household and the community are food insecure, it is the female children who pay the highest price in terms of malnutrition, because of gender discrimination.

Women farmers in the Global South are predominantly small-scale farmers. The partnership between women and biodiversity has kept the world fed throughout history, and will continue to feed the world in the future. It is this partnership that needs to be preserved and promoted to ensure food security.

Agriculture based on diversity, decentralization, and improving small-farm productivity through ecological methods is a women-centered, nature-friendly agriculture. In this women-centered agriculture, knowledge is shared, other species and plants are kin, not "property," and sustainability is based on the renewal of the Earth's fertility. Women's farming and knowledge are deeply tied to the emerging scientific paradigm of agroecology, where there is no place for monocultures of genetically engineered crops or a ruthless economics that seeks to destroy rather than conserve.

The future of food needs to be reclaimed by women, shaped by women, and democratically controlled by women. Only when food is in women's hands will both food and women be secure.

In 1996 Maria Mies and I initiated the Leipzig Appeal for Food Security in Women's Hands. Women worldwide are resisting the corporate control over food systems and creating alternatives to guarantee food security for their communities. Some of these are:

- Localization and regionalization instead of globalization
- Nonviolence instead of aggressive domination
- Equity and reciprocity instead of competition
- Respect for the integrity of nature and her species
- Understanding humans as part of nature instead of as masters over nature
- Protection of biodiversity in production and consumption

Here are some extracts from the text of the appeal:

For thousands of years women have produced their own food and guaranteed food security for their children and communities. Even today, 80 percent of the work in local food production in Africa is done by women, in Asia [it is] 50 to 60 percent and in Latin America [the number is] 30 to 40 percent.

Our food security is too vital an issue to be left in the hands of a few transnational corporations with their profit motives, or up to national governments that increasingly lose control over food security decisions, or to a few, mostly male national delegates at UN conferences, who take decisions affecting all our lives.

Food security must remain in women's hands everywhere! And men must share the necessary work, be it paid or unpaid. We have a right to know what we eat.... We will resist those who force us to produce and consume in ways that destroy nature and ourselves.[19]

9

The Way Forward

We stand at a watershed in terms of the interconnected future of food, people, and the planet.

If we continue down the path of industrial agriculture, GMOs, toxic chemicals, and corporate control, any benefits from them will be illusory. There will be an illusion of more food through the conversion of farmland to monoculture commodity production spaces. There will be an illusion of prosperity with more money flow, even though most money will be flowing away from farmers as their seed, land, and water are commodified, as their dependence on costly inputs deepens, and as their dependence on purchased food grows.

In the short run, more small-scale farmers who really feed the world will be displaced, more people will be hungry and suffer from diseases related to bad food, the deepening of the ecological crisis will threaten our very existence, and the erosion of food democracy will lead to the emergence of a food dictatorship.

In the long run, we will create conditions for our extinction as a species.

As I have written earlier, only 30 percent of the food eaten by people comes from large-scale industrial farms; 70 percent comes from small, biodiverse farms. On the other hand, 75 percent of the ecological destruction of our soil, water, and biodiversity is caused by industrial methods of farming, and 40 percent of the climate havoc we see today is caused by industrial globalized agriculture. Ecological unraveling is a nonlinear phenomenon, taking place according to an exponential curve of rapid change. Even if one assumes it is linear, by the time industrial agriculture can provide even 40 percent of our food supply, it will have destroyed 100 percent of our ecological life-support base. This is a recipe for extinction, not for feeding the world.

Extinction need not be our fate.

The model of agriculture based on diversity, democracy, and decentralization that is already contributing to 70 percent of the food that nourishes people can be increased to 100 percent. Through this process, we can heal and rejuvenate the planet, bring prosperity to farmers and the countryside, end agrarian distress and displacement, improve people's health, nutrition, and well-being, increase livelihood opportunities, and create more just, robust, and resilient economies.

So how do we get from here to there?

A nonsustainable, unhealthy, unjust, and undemocratic food system has been designed according to the Law of Exploitation by chemical corporations whose origins lie in war. But an ecologically sustainable, healthy, socially just, honest, and democratic food system aligned with the Law of Return is being advocated for and created by citizens everywhere. The specificities vary according to context, but the principles of the transition and of the emerging design are commonly shared.

It is these common principles of transition that are the key to making an ecological and democratic food system a 100 percent reality for all people on the planet. For this we need a road map to transition from a corporate-driven and corporate-controlled industrialized and globalized paradigm to an Earth-centered and people-centered paradigm of agroecology and food democracy. Here, I will divide this transition process into nine steps.

The first transition is from fiction to reality. We need to move from the fiction of corporate personhood to the reality of real people who grow, process, cook, and eat real food. From small-scale farmers to gardeners to mothers to children, these are real people with real bodies and real minds, who can cocreate and coproduce with nature. These are also real people who go hungry when they have no access to food and who suffer from diseases like obesity, diabetes, hypertension, cardiovascular diseases, and cancers when the food they eat is toxic and junk food.

Real people are creating real food systems that protect the Earth and serve people. Against all odds, people are designing new food systems that are the driving force behind this transition. Farming and gardening are becoming new revolutions. Whereas the rise of industrial agriculture was based on the removal of people from the land, the emergence of the new agriculture paradigm is based on returning to the dirt, to the Earth, and to the soil: in cities and in schools, on terraces and on walls. There is no person who cannot grow food, and part of being fully human is reconnecting to the Earth and its communities.

The second transition is from mechanistic, reductionist science to an agroecological science based on relationships and interconnectedness. It is the recognition that soil, seed, water, farmers, and our bodies are intelligent beings, not dead matter or machines. An expertise based on the violence of war is not relevant for evolving this intelligence, and it is not relevant to feeding people or to rejuvenating the planet. This intelligence is in the soil and in the seed; it is in the plants and in the animals; it is in our hands and in our bodies. The old universities teaching chemical warfare as agricultural expertise are being replaced by farms serving as schools, where the knowledge of real farming to produce real food is growing. A transition away from the rule of corporations and profits is also a knowledge transition toward the emerging scientific paradigm of agroecology.

The third transition is from seed as the "intellectual property" of corporations to seed as living, diverse, and evolving: toward seed as the commons that is the source of food and the source of life. The creation of community seed banks and seed libraries is part of the movements for seed freedom that are resisting the imposition of unscientific and unjust seed laws based on uniformity. Also part of this resistance are the scientific movements innovating with participatory and evolutionary breeding, which are offering successful and superior alternatives to industrial breeding.

The fourth transition is from chemical intensification to biodiversity intensification and ecological intensification, and from monocultures to diversity. We must make the transition from chemicals and toxins as the main input into agriculture to chemical-free, agroecological systems. The evidence that ecological systems produce more food and nutrition is growing. Chemicals have no place in farming and our food. This transition must also move away from the fiction of "high yield" to the reality of diverse systems outputs, including quantity, quality, taste, health, and nutrition. Not only are biodiverse agricultural systems more productive and resilient, biodiverse food systems are the best insurance against diseases linked to nutritional deficiencies. For example, the Indian science of Ayurveda demonstrates that all food should have six tastes, which ensures both diversity and health.

The fifth transition is from pseudoproductivity to real productivity. The reduction of living nature and creative people to "land," "labor," and mere inputs into the industrial system is a system of pseudoproductivity based on the Law of Exploitation. Rejuvenating natural resources and creating meaningful work and sustainable livelihoods are objectives and outputs of good farming, and cannot be reduced to inputs. In the pseudoproductivity calculus, the logic is to minimize labor input to make productivity increase. This means displacing farmers. In a real productivity calculus—one that is based on the real, not on the abstract—creative work is maximized as an output to increase productivity. Real productivity must internalize all social, health, and ecological costs of chemical-, capital-, and fossil-fuel-intensive industrial agriculture, as well as the benefits of ecological agriculture for public health, social cohesion, and ecological sustainability. A real productivity calculus recognizes farmers' rights. In an ecological and living world, farmers are not just producers of food; they are conservators and builders of biodiversity and a stable climate, they are providers of health, and they are the custodians of our diverse and collective cultures.

The most significant transition in our times is to decommodify and liberate land and labor, and focus on the living intelligence of nature, with her diversity and potential for creating abundance. We must also shift the focus to creative, intelligent, hardworking people who have rights to their land, their seed, their knowledge, creative work, and the fruits of their creative work through the Law of Return. This transition is being shaped by diverse movements working for the recognition of Mother Earth's rights, as well as the rights of all human beings to participate intelligently and democratically in the food web.

The sixth transition is from fake food to real food, from food that destroys our health to food that nourishes our bodies and minds. This is also a transition from food as a commodity produced for profits to food as the most important source of health and well-being. The entire food and agricultural system treats food as a commodity to be produced, processed, and traded solely to maximize corporate profits. The highest use value of food is in providing health and nourishment, and the primary contribution of food is to public health, not corporate profits. Commodities are based on quantity alone, irrespective of whether they are nutritionally empty or full of toxins and poisons. Food as a tradable commodity loses its use value of nourishment.

Really challenging the dominant food system involves nurturing the capacity to grow real, diverse food, creating innovative systems to distribute fresh and healthy food locally, and cultivating awareness about the difference between real food and fake food. This involves the right to know what you are eating, the right to choose ecologically sustainable, healthy, and safe food, and as a society the right to institutions for research and regulation that are independent of industry. Since the threat to the right to safe food comes through unjust and undemocratic laws, noncooperation with such laws through a Satyagraha—a fight for truth—becomes an ethical and a political imperative. This is what we did in Navdanya through the Sarson (Mustard) Satyagraha when our cold-pressed edible oils, including mustard oil, were banned so that markets could be flooded through dumping with GMO soy oil. Because of our actions and movements, cold-pressed mustard oil was not banned. The movement for chemical-free and GMO-free food that has exploded in recent times is based on people making a choice for health and safety. There is a new politics of food safety emerging as citizens rise up everywhere against poisons in our food and against the imposition of GMOs.

The seventh transition is from the obsession with "big" to a nurturing of "small," from the global to the local. Large-scale, long-distance food chains in an industrialized, globalized food system must become a small-scale, short-distance food web based on the ecological enlightenment that no place is too small to produce food. Everyone is an eater, and everyone has the right to healthy, safe food with the smallest ecological footprint. Everyone can also be a grower of food, which means that food can and must be grown everywhere.

We need food everywhere, and everywhere food will be different. Food in the Arctic will be different from food in a desert, which will be different from food in regions with high rainfall. Food in temperate regions will be different from food in tropical climates. To have food grown everywhere, there must be a transition from the resource- and energy-intensive, large-scale industrial agriculture model to ecologically adapted, small-scale, diverse systems. This adaptation and evolution, especially in response to climate change, will be vital to any sustainable food system in the future.

A frequently used argument is that we need large-scale industrial farms because more people are living in cities. This argument can be countered in three ways. First, large-scale farms are not producing food;

they are producing commodities. Commodities do not feed people. Second, every city should have its own "foodshed" that supplies most of its food needs in the same way that cities have "watersheds" that supply its water. Larger cities can have larger foodsheds. Planning for food needs, as well as integrating the city and the countryside through good food, should be part of urban planning. Third, the new food and agricultural movement is exploding in cities. Urban communities are reclaiming the food system through urban gardens, community gardens, school gardens, and gardens on terraces and balconies and walls. No place is too small to nourish a plant that can nourish us.

We are also told that more globalization and more corporate control over the food system are the solution to rising food prices and food inflation. This is false. A safe, affordable, diverse, and sustainable food system requires a transition from globalization to localization. The last two decades have seen the imposition of a globalized food system shaped and controlled by corporations with only one objective: profits. The Earth and her people have lost everywhere. The ecological crisis has deepened, and public health has worsened. Farmers are in distress. Localization, on the other hand, is the trend being shaped by movements for food democracy. Localization is expressed through urban gardens, farmers' markets, zero kilometer initiatives, and community-supported agriculture (CSA) initiatives, where people in cities can buy food directly from farmers. Local means diversity, freshness, safety, and taste. It means support for local farmers and it means rejuvenation of local economies. It means deeper connections between food producers and eaters, and it means cultivating not just food, but community. Localization means taking back our food through food democracy.

The eighth transition is from false, manipulated, and fictitious prices based on the Law of Exploitation to real and just prices based on the Law of Return. In rich countries, citizens are questioning "cheap" food and what an overconsumption of this food means for people's health. In poor countries, there are riots and protests and changes in regimes because of rising prices of food linked to free market policies. The Egyptian "Arab Spring," for example, started because of the rising prices of bread. Both the "cheap" food in rich countries and the rising costs of food in poor countries are based on a food system that puts profits above the rights of people to healthy, safe, and affordable food. This is based on the manipulation of prices by corporate giants and financial institutions through subsidies in rich countries, financial speculation, and betting on agriculture. Fair trade initiatives, on the other hand, allow farmers to get a fair and just return for their contributions to health and planetary care.

The price of anything should reflect its true cost and true benefits: the high costs of ecological degradation and damage to people's health in the case of chemical-intensive industrial agriculture, and the positive contributions of ecological agriculture to rejuvenating the soil, conserving biodiversity and water, mitigating climate change, and providing healthy, nutritious food.

We need to decommodify food and return it to its dignity. We must also return the dignity of the poorest to have the right to food. The value of food is in the nourishment, culture, and justice that it embodies. The value of food cannot be determined by a global casino. The true value and true price of food need to be based on the Law of Return, through a food democracy that reasserts the centrality of good, healthy, and affordable food to the life and health of every species on the planet.

The ninth transition is from the false idea of competition to the reality of cooperation. The entire edifice of industrial production, free trade, and globalization is based on competition as a virtue, as an essential human trait. Plants are put into competition with one another and with insects, including pollinators. Farmers are pitted against one another and against consumers, and every country is in competition with every other country through chasing investment performance and through trade wars. Competition creates a downward spiral from the perspective of the planet and people, and an upward spike for corporate profits. But the ultimate consequence of competition is collapse.

The reality of the web of life is cooperation: from the tiniest cell and microorganism to the largest mammal. Cooperation between diverse species increases food production and controls pests and weeds. Cooperation between people creates communities and living economies that maximize human welfare, including livelihoods, and minimize industry's profits. Cooperative systems are based on the Law of Return. They create sustainability, justice, and peace. In times of collapse, cooperation is a survival imperative.

These transitions are not a false utopia; they are actually taking place across the world. And emerging from the broken food system and the broken political system is a new living food system based on living seed, living soil, living food, and living farmers. For us, this transition process has been lived through the Navdanya movement for the last thirty years.

At Navdanya, we are the change we want to see in the world. Diversity, self-organization, cooperation, and the Law of Return have guided our work at every level. Diversity is the means and the end of everything we do, from conserving the biodiversity of plants and seeds, to resurrecting the diversity of knowledge systems, to creating biodiverse living economies, and to shaping a living food democracy.

Organic is not a "thing"; it is not a product. It is a philosophy: a way of thought and a way of living, based on the awareness that everything is connected, and everything is in a relationship with everything else. What we eat affects biodiversity, soil, water, climate, and farmers. What we do to the soil and the seed affects our own bodies and our health.

Navdanya means "nine seeds" and it also means "new gift." Nine seeds stands for diversity, and new gift stands for the seeds of life, freedom, and hope we plant. For us, seeds are a commons, not the invention and the patented property of a corporation. Navdanya began with the simple commitment to protect biodiversity and save seeds to keep them free from genetic engineering and patents. Today, more than three thousand varieties of rice have been conserved in the more than one hundred community seed banks started by Navdanya. The community seed banks were not designed to be a museum; they are living seed banks, an open source supply of seeds for the community, and seeds that different farming communities can freely exchange among themselves. Seeds and communities are not static; they evolve and change, and farmers as seed savers are also breeders who have bred seeds and plants for thousands of years. Living seeds evolve according to changes in the climate, and are therefore our best insurance against climate change.

For us, environment, poverty, and health are not separate from one another: they are different dimensions of an interconnected living food system—a food web, which is the web of life. For us, the seed, the soil, and the small-scale farmers are a continuum of creativity and productivity. From "seed to table" we work to protect and rejuvenate nature, farmers' lives, people's health, and social well-being by connecting the producer with the eater. There are four crucial links in Navdanya's "seed to table" cycle.

The first link is **living seeds** and the more than one hundred women-run community seed banks where we conserve and distribute seeds of diversity, including "forgotten foods" such as millets like *mandua* and *jhangora* and dals like *gahat* and *naurangi,* which are far more nutritious than the chemical monocultures of wheat and rice on which the Green Revolution depends. They also require ten times less water than industrially bred varieties. Through three decades of dedication, we have saved three thousand rice varieties and 150 wheat varieties. This is reversing the erosion of seed diversity and resisting the emergence of seed monopolies. We have challenged, and won cases against, the biopiracy of neem, basmati, and gluten-free wheat. Seeds are not things. They are the embodiment of centuries of evolutionary intelligence, and they hold within them the potential of thousands of years of creative evolution. Living seeds are the basis of an ecological agriculture based on biodiversity, not monocultures.

Our second link in the food chain is to join the living seed and the **living soil** through biodiversity-based organic farming. Seed makes soil and soil makes seed in a mutually beneficial, ever-renewing cycle based on the Law of Return. Industrial agriculture only measures what leaves the farm; we measure what is returned to the soil. Rejuvenating healthy soils has allowed us to increase productivity. It has also increased the water-holding capacity of the soil while reducing water demand.

In 1994 I started the Navdanya farm in Ramgarh village in my native Doon Valley on land that had been left barren by a eucalyptus plantation. Eucalyptus planting on farmland was promoted by the World Bank as "social forestry," but there was nothing social about it. Eucalyptus was selected only because it could be sold as raw material for the paper and pulp industry. It can be harvested in cycles of six years, and needs no active care before it is sold for pulping. It does, however, have huge water demands and leaves the soil barren because it does not return organic matter to the soil. In Australia, its native habitat, the aboriginal people managed the land through a fire cycle to recycle the eucalyptus leaves and their nutrients, making the continent the biggest garden on Earth. In India, these cycles are not a part of the ecosystem.

Today, this land is fertile, with earthworm castings everywhere. The water-holding capacity has increased so much that irrigation has been reduced by 75 percent. There is diversity everywhere: below the soil in the form of soil organisms and above the soil in the form of plants and pollinators. Instead of one nonfood species, we are growing more than two thousand varieties of crops, and more than 150 tree species. Just the mango grove has nine varieties of mangoes. A recent study has shown that there are six times more pollinators on the farm than in forests. And the two thousand varieties of crops we grow have increased both ecological balance and productivity on the farm. Soil fertility comes from the recycling of the organic matter on the farm, and pest management is carried out by the diversity of plants and insects. We do not have to spray poisons.

We have taken care of the Earth and brought back her biodiversity, thus increasing the capacity of the Earth to give us food. The land in Ramgarh carries two histories and two paradigms of agricultural land use: one symbolized by the eucalyptus monoculture and characterized by greed, profits, commerce, and carelessness, and the other driven by care for the Earth, and a respect for biodiversity and ecological processes. It is the second, agroecological model that has sustained us.

The third link is **living food economies.** Industrial farming and GMOs have trapped our farmers into a suicide economy. Globally, half of the one billion people who are hungry are farmers, because industrial globalized agriculture is based on the Law of Exploitation: it exploits both farmers and the land. We are creating living food economies based on diversity and the Law of Return, which ensures that farmers give back to the soil, and society gives back to the farmers.

Diversity and decentralization go hand in hand. That is why living food economies must be built on the foundation of local food economies. In linking seed to table, we have facilitated cooperation between producers and eaters through fair trade. We work with farming communities to form producer groups that fix their own prices and shape a just market. In this way, they are not pushed into competition with each other only to be exploited by an unfair, unjust market.

Since every person has a fundamental right to eat well, we link the rural areas to the cities through organic fair trade. The so-called "free trade" of globalization is free only for giant corporations. For citizens, it translates into participation through slavery or exclusion. Globalization has pitted consumers against farmers. At Navdanya, we have created cooperation between producers and eaters, and between the city and the countryside. We refer to our urban members as coproducers, because in choosing to eat biodiverse organic food, they are becoming partners with farmers in the act of conserving biodiversity and producing good food. Navdanya has four retail outlets in Delhi and one in Mumbai. We also run an organic café, where people can taste forgotten foods.

Cities can be producers too. That is why we have started Gardens of Hope in schools and in communities. Through gardening, every child becomes a potential farmer: a child of the Earth, a creator. We have also started Gardens of Hope with widows of farmers who have committed suicide in Punjab and Vidarbha. Through Gardens of Hope, people learn what it means to be a member of Vasudhaiva Kutumbakam, the Earth Family. When it comes to the Earth, we are all her children. Every person, rich or poor, young or old, of every creed and every caste, should learn to grow food. Every community space, every balcony, and every terrace should become a garden.

Growing organic in farms and gardens everywhere needs to become humanity's planetary mission. We have witnessed decades of a destructive agriculture that has wiped out biodiversity, desertified the soil, exhausted the water, polluted the air, and poisoned our bodies. We are innovating for a food and agricultural system that rejuvenates the Earth, our community, our cities, and our health.

For Navdanya, the fourth link in our work is **seeds of knowledge.** Bija Vidyapeeth—the Earth University—on the Navdanya farm in the Doon Valley is a learning center for spreading knowledge systems based on learning from nature. Its foundations are from centuries of the evolution of indigenous knowledge from women, from our grandmothers, and from teachers across the world. We call our farmers cocreators, since they work with the Earth, not against her. Navdanya farmers have trained and reached 750,000 farmers to practice an agriculture that protects the Earth, rebuilds soil, enhances food production, and increases rural incomes.

Seed sovereignty is linked to food sovereignty and to knowledge sovereignty. Every person is an expert in the knowledge they receive through their lived experience. A fragmented, reductionist paradigm does not just fragment reality. By creating a class of reductionist experts, it subjugates the diverse living knowledge systems that we need to redesign the broken food system.

Diverse Women for Diversity and Navdanya's Mahila Anna Swaraj (women's food sovereignty) programs put food safety, food security, and food sovereignty back into women's hands. The food products that women process are unique not only because of their gentle processing and light carbon footprints, but also because of their authentic and distinctive taste. These are sold from the shelves of our direct marketing outlets. Artisanal foods create employment, and they are a healthy alternative to industrial junk food. In fact, the WHO recently suggested that there should be a "health tax" levied on the junk-food industry.

Our work at Navdanya shows that we must make peace with the planet to address hunger. At Navdanya, we do not grow commodities; we grow the Earth community: in the mind and on the land. We feed the soil organisms, and they feed us. We grow diversity, which supports more diversity. The pest/predator balance this creates helps control pests, and we have no need to spray poisons. We grow organic matter, and return as much as we can to the soil. The organic matter in the soil is the alternative to the violence of fertilizer factories and the violence of large dams. Biodiverse systems increase resilience in times of climate chaos. The more biodiverse a system is, the more it is able to produce nutrition per acre and health per acre for eaters and wealth per acre for farmers.

I have built Navdanya over the last three decades to create a food and agricultural system that is at peace with the Earth. Nonviolent farming that protects species also helps us grow more food. And it produces better food, thus ending the war against our bodies that has led to the diseases of obesity, diabetes, hypertension, and cancers.

The same technological and economic systems that violate the Earth also violate the rights of communities to their natural resources. When land, biodiversity, and water are reduced to tradable commodities and are privatized, not only are the rights of nature violated, but the rights of communities are also violated. Making peace with the Earth begins with a paradigm shift from the mechanistic ideas of the Earth as dead matter to the Earth as Gaia: a living planet, our mother.

Industrial agriculture and industrial food systems have brought us a triple crisis: a dying planet, diseased citizens, and debt-ridden farmers. Ecological and just alternatives have become an imperative.

Seed freedom and food freedom are the foundations for food democracy. Food democracy is the right of farmers to save and share seed and to practice poison-free agroecology. It is the right of farmers to have the freedom to grow and share diversity through diversified and fair markets. Food democracy is the right of all citizens to have access to healthy, nutritious, safe, affordable, culturally appropriate, and sustainably produced food. It is the right to know what is in our food. Alternatives based on food democracy are flowering everywhere.

But an industry that has gotten used to profits at any cost will do its best to prevent the flowering of these alternatives. Pseudosafety laws, fascist seed laws, and neoliberal policies and markets are preventing alternatives to a model that is in deep crisis. This is the moment that calls for Satyagraha: the fight for truth.

Let us be the change we want to see, and let us each contribute to the shift from a poisoned food system to a living food system. No farmer should commit suicide. No child should die of hunger. No one should be sick because of food. The Earth, and human beings as cocreators with the Earth, can provide good and healthy food in abundance for all. Let us put our collective creative energies to work designing a future of food that protects the planet by working with Mother Earth to protect our soil, seeds, and biodiversity, instead of declaring a war against her through globalized agriculture and its weapons of war.

By working according to nature's laws, we each have within us the seeds of potential to bring abundant and good food to everyone, down to the last child, the last woman, the last farmer, and the last living being.

When we come together in harmony, we can cultivate paradise on Earth.

Endnotes

INTRODUCTION

1 Marie-Monique Robin, *Our Daily Poison: From Pesticides to Packaging, How Chemicals Have Contaminated the Food Chain and Are Making Us Sick* (New York: New Press, 2014).

2 Mike Adams, "World Bank Warns of Food Riots as Rising Food Prices Push World Populations toward Revolt," *OpEdNews,* June 1, 2014, www.opednews.com/articles/World-Bank-warns-of-food-r-by-Mike -Adams-Food_Food-Agriculture-Org-FAO_Food-Contamination_Food -Crisis-140601-389.html, accessed June 21, 2014.

3 "Hungry for Land: Small Farmers Feed the World with Less Than a Quarter of All Farmland," *Grain,* May 28, 2014, www.grain.org /article/entries/4929-hungry-for-land-small-farmers-feed-the -world-with-less-than-a-quarter-of-all-farmland, accessed June 22, 2014.

4 "Report of the International Technical Conference on Plant Genetic Resources, Leipzig, Germany, 17–23 June 1996," Food and Agriculture Organization of the United Nations, Rome, 1996.

5 "Colony Collapse Disorder Progress Report," US Department of Agri-culture, June 2010, quoted in www.greenpeace.org/eu-unit/Global /eu-unit/reports-briefings/2013/130409_GPI-Report_BeesInDecline .pdf.

6 "Water Uses," *AQUASTAT,* Food and Agriculture Organization of the United Nations, 2014, www.fao.org/nr/water/aquastat/water_use /index.stm.

7 Vandana Shiva, *Earth Democracy* (Cambridge, MA: South End Press, 2005).

8 Vandana Shiva, *Soil Not Oil* (New Delhi: Women Unlimited, 2008), 97.

9 "Climate Change 2007: Synthesis Report," Intergovernmental Panel on Climate Change (IPCC), 2007, www.ipcc.ch/pdf/assessment-report/ar4 /syr/ar4_syr.pdf.

10 Vandana Shiva, "Poisoned Roots," *Asian Age,* February 26, 2014, http://
archive.asianage.com/columnists/poisoned-roots-591, accessed August 7,
2015.

CHAPTER 1

1 John Augustus Voelcker, *Report on the Improvement of Indian Agriculture*
(London: Eyre and Spottiswoode, 1893), 11.

2 Albert Howard, *The Agricultural Testament* (London: Oxford University
Press, 1940), 10.

3 Amartya Sen, *Poverty and Famines: An Essay on Entitlement and
Deprivation,* 1983, Oxford Scholarship Online, November 2003,
www.oxfordscholarship.com/view/10.1093/0198284632.001.0001
/acprof-9780198284635.

4 Vandana Shiva, *The Violence of the Green Revolution* (Dehra Dun, India:
Natraj, 2010).

5 Quoted in Lothar Schaffer, *Infinite Potential* (New York: Random House,
2013), 34.

6 Bruce H. Lipton, *The Biology of Belief* (Carlsbad, CA: Hay House, 2008),
31.

7 Mae-Wan Ho and Eva Sirinathsinghji, *Ban GMOs Now: Health and
Environmental Hazards, Especially in the Light of the New Genetics* (London: Institute of Science and Society, 2010), 27.

8 Richard Lewontin, *Biology as Ideology: The Doctrine of DNA* (New York:
HarperCollins, 1993), 22.

9 Lipton, *The Biology of Belief,* 11.

10 Marilyn Waring, *If Women Counted: A New Feminist Economics* (San
Francisco: HarperCollins, 1988), 25.

CHAPTER 2

1 "Prithvi-Sukta: Hymn to the Earth (Atharva Veda)," *JaiMaa.org,*
June 22, 2014, www.jaimaa.org/articles/prithvi-sukta-hymn-to-the
-earth-atharva-veda/.

2 Albert Howard, *The Soil and Health,* 1st ed. (New York: Devin-Adair,
1956), 11.

3 Shiva, *The Violence of the Green Revolution,* 104.

4 "The Economics of Land Degradation: A Global Initiative for Sustainable Land Management," *ELD* brochure, 2014.

5 David Pimentel, "Soil Erosion: A Food and Environmental Threat," *Environment, Development, and Sustainability* 8 (2006): 119–137.

6 Vandana Shiva, *The Vandana Shiva Reader* (Lexington: University Press of Kentucky, 2014), 243, https://books.google.co.in/books?id=IyfJBQAAQBAJ.

7 Louise Howard, *Sir Albert Howard in India* (London: Faber and Faber, 1953), xv.

8 Shiva, *Soil Not Oil,* 101–102.

9 Nyle C. Brady and Ray R. Weil, *Elements of the Nature and Properties of Soils,* 3rd ed. (Upper Saddle River, NJ: Prentice Hall, 2009).

10 Charles Darwin, *The Formation of Vegetable Mould through the Action of Worms* (London: John Murray, 1881).

11 Howard, *The Soil and Health,* 63.

12 Howard, *An Agricultural Testament,* 25.

13 "Of Soils, Subsidies and Survival: A Report on Living Soils," Greenpeace India Society, 2011, 12.

14 Shiva, *Soil Not Oil,* 101.

15 Richard Heinberg, *The Party's Over: Oil, War and the Fate of Industrial Societies* (Gabriola Island, BC: New Society), 2003.

16 "Living Soils Report," Greenpeace India, February 3, 2011, www.greenpeace.org/india/en/publications/The-Living-Soils-Report/.

17 Shiva, *The Violence of the Green Revolution,* 104.

18 Howard, *The Soil and Health,* xxv.

19 Ibid.

20 Ibid.

21 Howard, The Soil and Health, 64, 13.

22 "Palli Prakriti," *Bhoomi: Learning from Nature, Remembering Tagore* (New Delhi: Navdanya, 2012), 10.

CHAPTER 3

1 Howard, *The Soil and Health*, xix.

2 W. W. Fletcher, *The Pest War* (Oxford, UK: Blackwell, 1984), 1.

3 Rachel Carson, *Silent Spring* (Boston: Houghton Mifflin, 1962), 2.

4 Ibid., 35.

5 John S. Wilson and Tsunehiro Otsuki, "To Spray or Not to Spray: Pesticides, Banana Exports and Food Safety" (Washington, DC: Development Research Group, World Bank, 2002).

6 Vandana Shiva, Mira Shiva, and Vaibhav Singh, *Poisons in Our Food* (Dehra Dun, India: Natraj, 2012), 2.

7 J. Jeyaratnam, "Acute Pesticide Poisoning: A Major Global Health Problem," *World Health Statistics Quarterly* 43 (1990): 139–144.

8 "Crop Protection by Seed Coating," *Communications in Agricultural and Applied Biological Sciences* 70, no. 3 (2005): 225–229.

9 "Seed Treatment," International Seed Federation, June 13, 2014, www.worldseed.org/isf/seed_treatment.html.

10 Tom Philpott, "90 Percent of Corn Seeds Are Coated with Bayer's Bee-Decimating Pesticide," *Mother Jones,* May 16, 2014, www.motherjones.com/tom-philpott/2012/05/catching-my-reading-ahead-pesticide-industry-confab, accessed June 14, 2014.

11 V. Shiva, M. Shiva, and Singh, *Poisons in Our Food,* 23.

12 Will Allen, The War on Bugs (White River Junction, VT: Chelsea Green, 2008), 96.

13 V. Shiva, M. Shiva, and Singh, *Poisons in Our Food,* 11.

14 Ibid., 16.

15 "Bhopal: The World's Worst Industrial Disaster," Greenpeace, June 20, 2014, www.greenpeace.org/international/en/multimedia/slideshows/bhopal-the-world-s-worst-ind/.

16 K. Raja, "Short Notes on Bhopal Gas Tragedy," Preserve Articles, June 14, 2014, www.preservearticles.com/2012013022181/short-notes-on-bhopal-gas-tragedy.html.

17 "Health Effects of Agent Orange/Dioxin," *Make Agent Orange History,* June 14, 2014, http://makeagentorangehistory.org/agent-orange-resources/background/health-effects-of-agent-orange-dioxin/.

18 Kounteya Sinha, "Nearly 7 Lakh Indians Died of Cancer Last Year: WHO," *Times of India,* December 14, 2013, http://timesofindia .indiatimes.com/india/7-lakh-Indians-died-of-cancer-last-year-WHO /articleshow/27317742.cms, accessed June 14, 2014.

19 "Cancer: Fact Sheet N°297," World Health Organization, February 2014, www.who.int/mediacentre/factsheets/fs297/en/, accessed April 14, 2014.

20 Josef Thundiyil, Judy Stober, Nida Besbelli, and Jenny Pronczuk, "Acute Pesticide Poisoning: A Proposed Classification Tool," *Bulletin of the World Health Organization* 86, no. 3 (March 2008): 161–240, www.who.int /bulletin/volumes/86/3/07-041814/en/.

21 David Pimentel, "Environmental and Economic Costs of the Application of Pesticides in the US Environment," *Development and Sustainability* 7 (2005), 229–252.

22 Channa Jayasumana, Sarath Gunatilake, and Priyantha Senanayake, "Glyphosate, Hard Water and Nephrotoxic Metals: Are They the Culprits Behind the Epidemic of Chronic Kidney Disease of Unknown Etiology in Sri Lanka?" *International Journal of Environmental Research and Public Health* 11, no. 2 (2014): 2,125–2,147.

23 "Why Are Autism Spectrum Disorders Increasing?" Centers for Disease Control and Prevention, June 18, 2014, www.cdc.gov/features /autismprevalence/.

24 K. W. Richards, "Non Apis Bees as Crop Pollinators," *Revue Suisse de Zoologie* 100 (1993): 807–822.

25 "Pollinators 101," *Native Pollinators in Agriculture Project,* www .agpollinators.org/pollinators, accessed June 20, 2014.

26 Marshall Levin, "Value of Bee Pollination to United States Agriculture," *American Bee Journal* 124, no. 3 (1984): 184–186.

27 V. Shiva, M. Shiva, and Singh, *Poisons in Our Food,* 1.

28 Quoted in Shiva, *The Violence of the Green Revolution,* 97.

29 "Who Owns Nature? Corporate Power and the Final Frontier in the Commodification of Life," *ETC Group,* November 12, 2008, www .etcgroup.org/content/who-owns-nature, accessed June 14, 2014.

30 "Monsanto: A Corporate Profile," *Food and Water Watch,* April 8, 2013, www.foodandwaterwatch.org/factsheet/monsanto-a-corporate-profile /, accessed June 14, 2014.

31 Ibid.

32 Warren Cornwall, "The Missing Monarchs," *Slate,* January 29, 2014, www.slate.com/articles/health_and_science/science/2014/01/mon -arch_butterfly_decline_monsanto_s_roundup_is_killing_milkweed .html, accessed June 20, 2014.

33 Madhura Swaminathan and Vikas Rawal, "Are There Benefits from the Cultivation of Bt Cotton?" *Review of Agrarian Studies* 1, no. 1 (January–June 2011).

34 Charles Benbrook, "Impacts of Genetically Engineered Crops on Pesticide Use in the US—the First Sixteen Years," *Environmental Sciences Europe* 24 (2012).

35 Ibid.

36 Jorge Fernandez-Cornejo and Craig Osteen, "Managing Glyphosate Resistance May Sustain Its Efficacy and Increase Long-Term Returns to Corn and Soybean Production," *Amber Waves,* May 4, 2015,

37 http://www.ers.usda.gov/amber-waves/2015-may/managing-glyphosate -resistance-may-sustain-its-efficacy-and-increase-long-term-returns-to -corn-and-soybean-production.aspx#.VkhXIIS6FmB.

38 Jennifer H. Zhao, Peter Ho, and Hossein Azadi, "Benefits of Bt Cotton Counterbalanced by Secondary Pests? Perceptions of Ecological Change in China," *Environmental Monitoring and Assessment* 173, nos. 1–4 (2011), 985–994.

39 "Who Benefits from GM Crops? Feeding the Biotech Giants, Not the World's Poor," *Friends of the Earth International,* February 2009, www. foei.org/en/resources/publications/pdfs/2009/gmcrops2009exec.pdf, accessed June 14, 2014.

40 Linda Pressly, "Are Pesticides Linked to Health Problems in Argentina?" *BBC News Magazine,* May 14, 2014, www.bbc.co.uk/news /magazine-27373134, accessed June 25, 2014.

41 "Use of Pesticides in Brazil Continues to Grow," *GM Watch,* April 18, 2011, www.gmwatch.org/latest-listing/1-news-items/13072-use-of -pesticides-in-brazil-continues-to-grow, accessed June 14, 2014.

42 Benbrook, "Impacts of Genetically Engineered Crops on Pesticide Use in the US."

43 "Mike Mack on GMOs: 'There's Very Little about Farming That's Natural,'" *Huffington Post,* January 24, 2014, www.huffingtonpost

.com/2014/01/24/michael-mack-davos_n_4636222.html?utm_hp
_ref=food&ir=Food, accessed June 14, 2014.

44 Zeyaur Khan, David Amudavi, and John Pickett, "Push-Pull Technology Transforms Small Farms in Kenya," *PAN North America Magazine,* Spring 2008, www.push-pull.net/panna.pdf, accessed June 14, 2014.

45 Joko Mariyono, "Integrated Pest Management Training in Indonesia: Does the Performance Level of Farmer Training Matter?" *Journal of Rural and Community Development* 4, no. 2 (2009): 93–104.

46 "State to Promote Pesticide-Free Farming," *The Hindu,* November 21, 2004, www.hindu.com/2004/11/21/stories/2004112103040500.htm, accessed June 14, 2014.

47 "Pesticides and Honeybees: State of the Science," *Pesticide Action Network North America,* May 2012.

48 The Bee Coalition, "Myths and Truths about Neonicotinoids, Chemicals and the Pesticides Industry," www.buglife.org.uk/sites/default/files/The%20 bee%20coalition%202014%20Myths%20and%20truths%20about%20 neonicotinoids.pdf.

49 Charlotte McDonald-Gibson, "'Victory for Bees' as European Union Bans Neonicotinoid Pesticides Blamed for Destroying Bee Population," *The Independent,* April 29, 2013, www.independent.co.uk/environment /nature/victory-for-bees-as-european-union-bans-neonicotinoid -pesticides-blamed-for-destroying-bee-population-8595408.html, accessed June 20, 2014.

50 "Chinese Army Bans All GMO Grains and Oil from Supply Stations," *Sustainable Pulse,* May 14, 2014, http://sustainablepulse.com/2014 /05/14/chinese-army-bans-gmo-grains-oil-supply-stations/#.U6v1I -hY2nwI, accessed June 25, 2014.

51 "It's Official—Russia Completely Bans GMOs," *Collective Evolution,* April 15, 2014, www.collective-evolution.com/2014/04/15/its-official -russia-completely-bans-gmos/, accessed June 25, 2014.

CHAPTER 4

1 "Usefulness of and Threats to Plant Genetic Resources," *ADBInstitute,* June 5, 2014, www.adbi.org/working-paper/2009/10/15/3347 .biodiversity.organic.agriculture/usefulness.of.and.threats.to.plant .genetic.resources/.

2 B. J. Cardinale et al., "Biodiversity Loss and Its Impact on Humanity," *Nature* 486: 59–67.

3 "William Lockeretz," *US Department of Agriculture: Alternative Farming Systems Information Center,* June 20, 2014, http://afsic.nal.usda .gov/videos/histories/william-lockeretz.

4 Francesca Bray, "Agriculture for Developing Nations," *Scientific American,* July 1994: 33–35.

5 Ibid.

6 T. Cacek, "Organic Farming: The Other Conservation Farming System," *Journal of Soil and Water Conservation* 39 (1984): 357–360.

7 Charles Mann, *1491: New Revelations of the Americas before Columbus* (New York: Vintage Books, 2005), 197–198.

8 "Companion Planting: The Three Sisters," *Almanac.com,* June 5, 2014, www.almanac.com/content/companion-planting-three-sisters.

9 Vandana Shiva and Vaibhav Singh, "Health Per Acre" (New Delhi: Navdanya, 2011).

CHAPTER 5

1 Quoted in Vandana Shiva, *Yoked to Death: Globalisation and Corporate Control of Agriculture* (New Delhi: Research Foundation for Science, Technology and Ecology, 2001), 21.

2 Joel Dyer, *Harvest of Rage: Why Oklahoma City Is Only the Beginning* (Boulder, CO: Westview, 1998).

3 Quoted in Shiva, *Yoked to Death,* 24.

4 Charan Singh, *Economic Nightmare in India* (New Delhi: National Publishing House, 1984), 119.

5 National Crime Records Bureau, Ministry of Home Affairs, "Accidental Deaths & Suicides in India: 2014," http://ncrb.gov.in/ADSI2014/ADSI2014 .htm; P. Sainath, "Maharashtra Crosses 60,000 Farm Suicides," July 15, 2014, https://psainath.org/maharashtra-crosses-60000-farm-suicides.

6 "Why Are the FAO and the EBRD Promoting the Destruction of Peasant and Family Farming?" *Grain,* September 14, 2012, www.grain .org/article/entries/4572-why-are-the-fao-and-the-ebrd-promoting-the -destruction-of-peasant-and-family-farming, accessed June 15, 2014.

7 Shiva, *Yoked to Death*, 8–9.

8 "Wake Up Now before It Is Too Late: Make Agriculture Truly Sustainable Now for Food Security in a Changing Climate," *Trade and Environment Review 2013* (Geneva: UNCTAD, 2013).

9 Peter Rosset, "Small Is Bountiful," *The Ecologist* 29, no. 8 (December 1999).

10 International Labour Organization, "ILO and Cooperatives," *ILO COOP News,* no. 4 (2012).

11 "The State of Land in Europe," *Agrarian Justice,* April 14, 2014, www .tni.org/infographic/state-land-europe, accessed June 15, 2014.

12 Tom Philpott, "Wall Street Investors Take Aim at Farmland," *Mother Jones,* March 14, 2014, www.motherjones.com/tom-philpott/2014/03 /land-grabs-not-just-africa-anymore, accessed June 15, 2014.

13 "How Much Farmland Has India Lost?" *The Economic Times,* November 12, 2013, http://articles.economictimes.indiatimes.com/2013-11-12 /news/43981319_1_cultivable-land-agricultural-land-million-hectares, accessed June 25, 2014.

14 Quoted in Pyarelal, *Towards New Horizons* (Ahmedabad, India: Navajivan Press, 1959), 150.

15 Suma Chakrabarti and José Graziano da Silva, "Hungry for Investment: The Private Sector Can Drive Agricultural Development in Countries That Need It the Most," *Wall Street Journal,* September 6, 2012, http:// online.wsj.com/news/articles/SB10000872396390443686004577633080190871456?mg=reno64-wsj&url=http%3A%2F%2Fonline.wsj.com %2Farticle%2FSB10000872396390443686004577633080190871456 .html, accessed June 15, 2014.

CHAPTER 6

1 Vandana Shiva and Kunwar Jalees, *Seeds of Suicide* (New Delhi: Navdanya, 2006), 48.

2 Ibid., 2–3.

3 Ibid., 3.

4 Ibid., 75.

5 Translated from Quechua to English by William Rowe and quoted in Shiva, *The Violence of the Green Revolution*, 255.

6 "Agreement on Trade-Related Aspects of Intellectual Property Rights," World Trade Organization. April 15, 1994.

7 Food and Water Watch, 2013.

8 Vandana Shiva, *Stolen Harvest: The Hijacking of the Global Food Supply* (New Delhi: India Research Press, 2000), 93.

9 "'Gene Police' Raise Farmers' Fears," *Washington Post*, February 3, 1999: 2.

10 WTO Council for Trade Related Aspects of Intellectual Property Rights, IP/C/W/161, November 3, 1993.

11 WTO Council for Trade Related Aspects of Intellectual Property Rights, IP/C/W/404, June 26, 2003.

12 Shiva and Jalees, *Seeds of Suicide*, 25.

13 National Crime Records Bureau, Ministry of Home Affairs, "Accidental Deaths & Suicides in India: 2014"; P. Sainath, "Maharashtra Crosses 60,000 Farm Suicides."

14 Ibid., 246–247.

CHAPTER 7

1 Ethan A. Huff, "Consolidation of Seed Companies Leading to Corporate Domination of World Food Supply," *Natural News*, July 27, 2011, www .naturalnews.com/033148_seed_companies_Monsanto.html, accessed June 25, 2014.

2 Nigel Morris, "The Big Five Companies That Control the World's Grain Trade," *The Independent*, January 23, 2013, www.independent.co.uk /news/uk/home-news/the-big-five-companies-that-control-the-worlds -grain-trade-8462266.html, accessed June 25, 2014.

3 "Global Top 10 Food Companies: Company Guide," *Just Food*, Canada Ltd., November 2013.

4 "Leading Retailers," *Food Retail World*, June 25, 2014, www.foodretail -world.com/LeadingRetailers.htm.

5 Duncan Green and Matthew Griffith, "Dumping on the Poor: The Common Agricultural Policy, the WTO and International Development,"

CAFOD Trade Justice Campaign, September 2002, www.iatp.org/files /Dumping_on_the_Poor_The_Common_Agricultural_Po.htm, accessed June 15, 2014.

6 Kevin Watkins, "Northern Agricultural Policies and World Poverty: Will the Doha 'Development Round' Make a Difference?" Oxfam, 2003.

7 Green and Griffith, "Dumping on the Poor."

8 Vandana Shiva, Afsar H. Jafri, and Kunwar Jalees, *The Mirage of Market Access: How Globalisation Is Destroying Farmers' Lives and Livelihoods* (New Delhi: Navdanya/Research Foundation for Science and Technology, 2003), 25.

9 "An Answer to the Global Food Crisis: Peasants and Small Farmers Can Feed the World!" La Via Campesina: International Peasant's Movement, May 1, 2008, http://viacampesina.org/en/index.php/main-issues-main menu-27/food-sovereignty-and-trade-mainmenu-38/505-an-answer-to -the-global-food-crisis-peasants-and-small-farmers-can-feed-the-world, accessed June 15, 2014.

10 Ibid.

11 Shiva, Jafri, and Jalees, *The Mirage of Market Access,* 63.

12 Quoted in Shiva, *Yoked to Death,* 40.

13 Frederick Kaufman, "How Wall Street Starved Millions and Got Away with It," *Harper's Magazine,* July 2010.

14 Food and Agriculture Organization of the United Nations, *The State of Food Insecurity in the World,* 2012.

15 "Where Does Hunger Exist?" Bread for the World Institute, www.bread .org.

16 Jenny Hope, "Hunger in Britain Is Becoming 'Public Health Emergency' as Number of People Turning to Food Banks to Feed Families Soars," *Daily Mail,* December 4, 2013, www.dailymail.co.uk/news /article-2517898/Hunger-Britain-public-health-emergency-number -people-turning-food-banks-feed-families-soars.html, accessed June 15, 2014.

17 "EPAs: Through the Lens of Kenya," *Traidcraft and EcoNews Africa,* 2005, www.traidcraft.co.uk/Resources/Traidcraft/Documents/PDF/tx /campaigns_epas_free_trade_wont_help_africa.pdf.

18 "Kenya," *Food Security Portal,* June 20, 2014, www.foodsecurityportal .org/kenya?print.

19 "Kenya's Food Exports vs. Food Aid," *Koru Kenya,* August 1, 2013, http://koru.or.ke/Kenyas_Food_Exports_vs_Food_Aid, accessed June 20, 2014.

20 Samuel L. Aronson, "Crime and Development in Kenya: Emerging Trends and Transnational Implications of Political, Economic, and Social Instability," *Student Pulse* 2, no. 9 (2009), www.studentpulse.com /articles/278/2/crime-and-development-in-kenya-emerging-trends-and -the-transnational-implications-of-political-economic-and-social -instability, accessed June 20, 2014.

21 "EPAs: Through the Lens of Kenya."

22 Government of Kenya, *The 2003–2007 Economic Recovery Strategy for Wealth and Employment Creation,* June 2003, xiii.

23 Emilio Godoy, "Drugs Displace Maize on Mexico's Small Farms," *Inter Press Service,* January 22, 2014, www.ipsnews.net/2014/01/drugs -displace-maize-mexicos-small-farms/, accessed June 20, 2014.

24 Matthew Davis, "Globalization and Poverty in Mexico," *National Bureau of Economic Research,* www.nber.org/digest/apr05/w11027.html, accessed June 20, 2014.

25 Ibid.

26 Elvia R. Arriola, "Accountability for Murder in the Maquiladoras: Linking Corporate Indifference to Gender Violence at the US-Mexico Border," *Seattle Journal for Social Justice* 5, no. 2 (Spring/Summer 2007).

27 Food and Agriculture Organization of the United Nations, *The State of Food Insecurity in the World: Economic Crises—Impacts and Lessons Learned,* 2009, 11.

28 Report of the UN Special Rapporteur on the Right to Food, p. 3, www.srfood.org/images/stories/pdf/officialreports/20101021_access-to -land-report_en.pdf.

29 Development Education, www.developmenteducation.ie.

30 Adams, "World Bank Warns of Food Riots."

31 Food and Agriculture Organization of the United Nations, www.fao.org /es/esc/prices/CIWP.

32 Vandana Shiva and Kunwar Jalees, *Why Is Every 4th Indian Hungry? The Causes and Cures for Food Insecurity* (New Delhi: Navdanya, 2009), 1.

33 Ibid.

34 Ibid.

35 Department of Biology, University of Indiana, "Obesity, Type 2 Diabetes and Fructose," August 24, 2010, www.indiana.edu/~oso/Fructose/Fructose.html, accessed June 20, 2014.

36 George A. Bray, Samara Joy Nielsen, and Barry M. Popkin, "Consumption of High-Fructose Corn Syrup in Beverages May Play a Role in the Epidemic of Obesity," *American Journal of Clinical Nutrition* 79, no. 4 (2004): 537–543.

37 "Annual Financials for PepsiCo Inc.," MarketWatch, https://secure.marketwatch.com/investing/stock/PEP/financials#.

38 PepsiCo website, www.pepsico.com.

39 Shiva, *Stolen Harvest*, 70; Alex Hershaft, "Academy of Science Confirms Diet–Cancer Link," *Vegetarian Times*, September 1982: 7–8, https://books.google.ae/books?id=hQcAAAAAMBAJ.

40 Vandana Shiva, "The Wrong Choice, Baby?" *Asian Age*, December 4, 2013, http://dc.asianage.com/columnists/wrong-choice-baby-873, accessed June 22, 2014.

41 "India Likely to Beat China to Become Diabetes Capital in the World," *Silicon India*, June 13, 2014, www.siliconindia.com/news/life/India-Likely-To-Beat-China-To-Become-Diabetes-Capital-In-The-World-nid-167867-cid-51.html, accessed June 15, 2014.

42 "Furor on Memo at World Bank," *New York Times Archives*, February 7, 1992, www.nytimes.com/1992/02/07/business/furor-on-memo-at-world-bank.html, accessed June 22, 2014.

43 Shiva, *Soil Not Oil*, 103.

44 Stephen Bentley and Ravenna Barker, "Fighting Global Warming at the Farmers' Market," *FoodShare Research in Action Report*, FoodShare Toronto, 2005.

45 Tim Lang and Michael Heasman, *Food Wars: The Global Battle for Mouths, Minds and Markets* (London: Earthscan, 2004), 235–238.

46 Andy Jones, *Eating Oil: Food in a Changing Climate* (London: Sustain/ELM Farm Research Center, 2001), 13.

47 Tracy Worcester, "Local Food," *Resurgence* 199 (March/April 2000).

48 Food and Agriculture Organization, "Toolkit: Reducing the Food Wastage Footprint," www.fao.org/docrep/018/i3342e/i3342e.pdf.

49 Ibid.

50 National Crime Records Bureau, Ministry of Home Affairs, "Accidental Deaths & Suicides in India: 2014"; P. Sainath, "Maharashtra Crosses 60,000 Farm Suicides."

CHAPTER 8

1 Food and Agriculture Organization of the United Nations, "Women's Contributions to Agricultural Production and Food Security: Current Status and Perspectives," www.fao.org/docrep/x0198e/x0198e02.htm, accessed June 22, 2014.

2 J. Spedding et al., eds., *The Works of Francis Bacon*, vol. V (Stuttgart, Germany: F. F. Verlag, 1963), 506.

3 Quoted in Evelyn Fox Keller, *Reflections on Gender and Science* (New Haven, CT: Yale University Press, 1985), 7.

4 Quoted in Brian Easlea, *Science and Sexual Oppression: Patriarchy's Confrontation with Women and Nature* (London: Weidenfeld and Nicholson, 1981), 64.

5 Ibid., 70.

6 Ibid., 73.

7 Carolyn Merchant, *The Death of Nature: Women, Ecology and the Scientific Revolution* (New York: Harper and Row, 2006), 182.

8 FAO, "Women Feed the World," 1998.

9 Vandana Shiva, *Staying Alive* (New Delhi: Kali Unlimited, 2010), x.

10 Ronnie Lessem and Alexander Schieffer, *Integral Economics* (Surrey, UK: Gower, 2010), 124.

11 Josh Clark, "Why Do Corporations Have the Same Rights as You?" *How Stuff Works*, www.howstuffworks.com/corporation-person1.htm, accessed June 15, 2014.

12 "Monsanto Sues Vermont, Claims First-Ever GMO Labeling Law in the US Violates Free Speech," *The Anti-Media,* June 16, 2014, http://theantimedia.org/monsanto-sues-vermont-claims-first-ever-gmo-labeling-law-in-u-s-violates-free-speech/, accessed June 18, 2014.

13 Doug Rushkoff, "Corporations as Uber-Citizens," *Rushkoff.com,* January 22, 2010, www.rushkoff.com/blog/2010/1/22/corporations-as-uber-citizens.html.

14 Amartya Sen, "More Than 100 Million Women Are Missing," *New York Review of Books,* December 20, 1990, www.nybooks.com/articles/archives/1990/dec/20/more-than-100-million-women-are-missing/, accessed June 17, 2014.

15 Shiva, *Staying Alive,* xvi.

16 Guangwen Tang, Jian Qin, Gregory G. Dolnikowski, Robert M. Russell, and Michael A. Grusak, "Golden Rice Is an Effective Source of Vitamin A," *American Journal of Clinical Nutrition* 89, no. 6 (2009): 1,776–1,783.

17 C. Gopalan et al., *Nutritive Value of Indian Foods* (Hyderabad, India: Indian Council of Medical Research, 2009).

18 Ibid.

19 Navdanya, "The Movement," www.navdanya.org/archives/20-the-movement, accessed June 18, 2014.

Index

A

Actinomycetes, 18–19
ADM (Archer Daniels Midland), 86, 92
Aelvoet, Magda, 38
Aeon, 86
African Biodiversity Network, 81
African Centre for Biosafety, 81
Agent Orange, 32, 34
Agroecology
  biodiversity and, 37
  knowledge paradigm of, x–xi, 3, 11–13
  meaning of, xviii–xix
  sustainability and, 9–10
  transitioning to, 126–33
Albrecht, Josef, 75
Algae, 19
American Cyanamid, 29
American Society for Clinical Nutrition, 103
Amstutz, Dan, 92
Arche Noah, 81
Argentina, 36
Arguedas, José María, 71
Arsenic, 30–31
Associazione Donne in Campo, 81
Autism, 32

B

Bacon, Francis, 113–14
Bacteria, in soil, 18–19, 21
Bananas, iron-enriched, 121, 122

Baranaaja, 51–52, 53
Basel AG, 29
BASF, 29
Bayer, xvii, 29, 30, 38, 39, 86
Bees. *See also* Pollinators
  decline in, xii, 33, 38–39
  importance of, xii, 33
  pesticides' effects on, 33, 38–39
Benbrook, Charles, 35–37
Bhopal gas tragedy, 31
Bija Satyagraha, 82
Bija Vidyapeeth, 137
Biodiversity
  cultural diversity and, 43, 52, 56
  culture practices based on, 51–53
  importance of, xix
  loss of, 42–44, 49–50
  pests and, 27, 37–38, 40, 41
  productivity and, 46–48, 50–51, 53–54
  small-scale farming and, 56
  sustainability and, 50
  transitioning to, 128
  women and, 115
Biofortification, 121–22
Bio nullius, 71, 77, 79
Biopiracy, 76–77
Bollgard, 35
Borg, Tonio, 39
Borlaug, Norman, xvi, 17, 119
Bowman, Vernon Hugh, 72–73

Boyle, Robert, 114
Brazil
    GMOs in, 36, 77
    pesticides in, 36
    small-scale farming in, 61
British Society of Plant Breeders, 75
Bt crops, 34, 35, 36, 63, 121
Bullard, Linda, 38
Bunge, 86, 92
Bush, George W., 101–2
Butterflies, 33, 35. *See also*
    Pollinators

C
Cameroon, ix
Canada, 58, 99, 106
Canadian National Farmers Union,
    59
Cargill, 86, 92, 94
Carrefour, 86
Carson, Rachel, 28, 29
Center for Food Safety, 81
Chakrabarti, Suma, 65
China
    food prices in, 102
    GMOs in, 36, 39
    growth of, 101–2
    history of agriculture in, 2
    hunger in, 101
    loss of fertile soil in, 16
CIMMYT (International Maize and
    Wheat Improvement Center),
    70, 119
Climate change
    globalization and, 105–6
    industrial agriculture and, xiii,
        8, 24
    pesticides and, 39
    synthetic fertilizers and, 21

Clinton, Bill, 99
Colombia, 61, 82
Common Agricultural Policy
    (CAP), 89
Competition, 6–7, 93–94
ConAgra, 92
Continental, 92
Corporations. *See also individual*
    corporations
    control of seed by, 42, 43
    domination by, 55
    globalization and, 86, 112–13
    greed of, xviii, 39
    militarized mindset of, 39–40
    "personhood" of, xiv–xv, xvii,
        117–18
    power of, xvii–xviii
Crotalaria, 20
Cruiser, 39
Cuesta, José, 101

D
Dale, James, 122
Danone, 86
Darwin, Charles, 6, 19
DeBach, Paul, 33–34
Descartes, René, 113
Devi, Susheela, 63
Dhaikan, 38
Diabetes, 103–4
Diverse Women for Diversity, 137
Domination, Law of, x, 34, 47–48
Dow, xvii, 31–32, 86
Dumping, 88–89
DuPont, xvii, 29, 86

E
Earthworms, 19, 21–22
East India Company, 86, 117

Einstein, Albert, xii
"Energy slaves," xiii, 22
Epigenetics, 5
ETC Group, 81
Eucalyptus, 49, 135
European Union
  agricultural subsidies in, 89
  pesticides in, 39
  seed laws in, 75, 82
  small-scale farming in, 61, 64
Exploitation, Law of
  effects of, ix–x, 24
  food chains and, 60–61
  monocultures and, 47–48
  transitioning from, 131–32

F
I. G. Farben, 29, 31
Fertilizers, synthetic
  effects of, xiii, 16, 21
  fossil fuels and, xii–xiii, 22
  global annual consumption of,
    21
  origins of, 7, 16, 20–21
Flagship, 39
Fondation Danielle Mitterrand, 81
Food and Agriculture Organization
  (FAO), 38, 60, 62, 65, 91, 96,
    106, 107, 120
Food and Water Watch, 34
Food chains vs. food webs, 60–61
Food democracy, 138–39
Food miles, 105–6
Food prices, 92–96, 101–2, 110,
    131–32
Food riots, ix, 101
Food safety laws, 76, 107
Food security, 47, 55–56, 97–100,
    107, 112, 124

Food sovereignty, xx, 12, 82, 108–9,
    137
Food waste, 106–7
Fossil fuels, xii–xiii, 22
France, 39
"Freedom," meaning of, 108–9
Frito-Lay, 104

G
Gandhi, Mahatma, 65, 75
Gardens of Hope, 136–37
Garlic, 38
Garnac, 92
Gates, Bill, xvi, 122
Gatorade, 104
Gaucho, 39
General Mills, 59
Genetic engineering. See also GMOs
  belief system behind, 5
  false claims of, 17, 47
  patents and, 71
Germany, 75, 93
Glanvill, Joseph, 114
Glencore International, 86
Globalization
  architects of, 92
  beneficiaries of, 88, 92
  climate change and, 105–6
  competition and, 93–94
  costs of, 87
  effects of, 56, 63–64, 86, 87–88,
    108–9, 110
  false claims for, 86–87
  food prices and, 92–96
  food waste and, 106–7
  history of, 86
  hunger and, 87–88, 96–102
  monopolies and, 86
  obesity and, 103–4

patriarchal economics and,
112–13
trade liberalization and, 88–91
transitioning from, 136
Glyphosate, 32, 35–36
Glyricidia, 20
GMOs (genetically modified
organisms)
bans on, 39
beneficiaries of, xvii
characteristics of, 69
claims for, xvii, 69
contamination by, 73, 77
effects of, 5, 32–33, 34–35,
125–26
labeling laws for, 117–18
manufacturers of, 34
pesticides and, 34, 35–37
production methods for, 69
purpose of, 69–70
royalty collection for, 77
terminator seeds, 69
W. R. Grace, 38
GRAIN, 81
Grain monopolies, 86, 92
Graziano da Silva, José, 65
Green manures, 20
Green Revolution
effects of, on soil, 16, 23
false claims of, xvi, 17
GMOs and, xvii
history of, xv–xvi
pesticides and, 32
productivity and, 46–47, 53
seeds and, 70, 119–20
Grocery Manufacturers Association
(GMA), 117–18
Grupo de Reflexión Rural, 81

H

Hayes, Tyrone, 33
Heinberg, Richard, 22
Helix, 39
HFCS (high fructose corn syrup),
103
Hitler, Adolf, 29
Ho, Mae-Wan, 5
Hoechst, 29
Honcho, 39
Howard, Albert, 2, 15, 17, 20–21,
23, 24, 25, 27
Hubbert, M. King, 22
Humus, 18, 23
Hunger, 87–88, 96–102, 109
Hybrid seeds, 68–69, 120
HYVs (high yielding varieties),
45–46, 50, 68

I

IFOAM (International Federation
of Organic Agriculture
Movements), 81
ILO (International Labour
Organization), 62
India
biodiversity in, 43, 51–52
diabetes in, 104
farmers' suicides in, 48, 60,
64–65, 78–79, 107
food prices in, 92–93, 101–2
food riots in, ix
food safety laws in, 76
globalization and, 88–89, 90
GMOs in, 35, 74, 121
Green Revolution in, xvi, 16, 17
growth of, 101–2
history of agriculture in, 1–2

hunger in, 101–2, 104, 107
loss of fertile soil in, 16
obesity in, 104
pesticides in, 30–31, 32, 38
pollution in, 105
seed coating in, 30
seed laws in, 82
small-scale farming in, 63, 64
vegetable oil production in, 90
Indonesia
 food prices in, 94–96
 integrated pest management in,
  38
 small-scale farming in, 62
 soy production in, 91, 94–95
Industrial agriculture. *See also*
  Monocultures
 climate change and, xiii, 8, 24
 effects of, xii–xv, 2, 44–45, 56,
  87–88, 125–26, 138
 false productivity of, xii, 44–49,
  56–57, 63, 92
 food prices and, 92–96
 pest control and, 28
 subsidies for, 87
 transitioning from, 130–31
 view of soil by, 23
 violent paradigm of, ix–x, xi–xii,
  3, 7–8, 113
International Fund for Agricultural
  Development, 91
IRRI (International Rice Research
  Institute), 70, 119

J
Jamaica, 89
Java, 61
JBS, 86

"Jobs," meaning of, 57
Junk food, xiii, 103–4, 137

K
Karanj, 38
Kazakhstan, 61
Kellogg's, 59
Kenya
 globalization's effects on, 97–99
 hunger in, 98
 small-scale farming in, 62
KFC (Kentucky Fried Chicken),
  104
Kissinger, Henry, 82
"Knowledge terrorism," 33
Kokopelli, 81
Kuhn, Thomas, 2

L
Lal, Mukundi, 63
Large-scale farming
 effects of, 8, 58–59
 productivity and, 57, 59, 60
Lee Kyung Hae, 78
Leipzig Appeal for Food Security in
  Women's Hands, 124
Lessem, Ronnie, 117
Lewontin, Richard, 5–6
Lipton, Bruce H., 6
Livelihoods
 destruction of, 58, 60
 devaluation of, 58
 meaning of, 57
Localization
 benefits of, 108
 importance of, xx, 85–86
 transitioning to, 109–10, 130–
  31, 136–37

Lockeretz, William, 48
Louis Dreyfus, 86, 92
Lovins, Amory, xiii

M
Mack, Mike, 37
Mahila Anna Swaraj, 137
Mann, Charles C., 52
Maquiladoras, 100
March against Monsanto, xvii
McDonald's, xiii, 42, 92, 104
Medvedev, Dmitry, 39
Merchant, Carolyn, 114
Metro Group, 86
Mexico
    biodiversity loss in, 42, 43, 73
    globalization's effects on, 99–100
    mixed farming in, 6
    monarch butterflies in, 35
Mies, Maria, 124
Milkweed, 35
Milpa, 52–53
Mishra, Shri Chaturanan, 81
Mitsui/Cook, 92
Monarch butterflies, 35
Monocultures
    competition and, 6
    food production by, 44, 45–49,
        115
    of the Mind, 43, 44–45, 113,
        121
    nonsustainability of, 49–50
    pests and, 27
    prevalence of, 41–42
    transitioning from, 128
Monsanto, xvii, 32, 34, 35, 69, 72–
    74, 77, 79, 86, 117–18, 121
Mycorrhizae, 18, 21
"Myth of more," 58, 59, 60, 87

N
NAFTA (North American Free
    Trade Agreement), 99–100
Navdanya (culture system), 51, 53
Navdanya (seed saving movement)
    goals of, xxi, 80, 133–34, 138
    inspiration for, 65
    naming of, 51, 133
    research by, 35, 53–54, 63, 78,
        108
    retail outlets of, 136
    "seed to table" cycle of, 134–38
    soil at, 23–24
Nayakrishi, 81
Neem, 38
Nematodes, 19
Neonicotinoids, 39
Nestlé, 86
Newton, Isaac, 4, 113
Nigeria, 62, 115
Nitrogen, 19–21, 22
Nitrous oxide, 21
No Patents on Seeds, 81
Nurgundi, 38

O
Obesity, 103–4
Oldenburg, Henry, 114
Organic farming
    father of, 15
    knowledge paradigm of, 3
    nitrogen-fixing crops and, 20
    productivity and, 48, 54
Organophosphates (OPs), 31
OSGATA (Organic Seed Growers
    and Trade Association), 81

P
Papua New Guinea, 61

Patriarchal economics, 112–13,
  116–19
"Peak oil," 22
PepsiCo, 42, 86, 92, 104
Perennia, 81
Pesticides
  bans on, 38–39
  categories of, 29
  coating seeds with, 30
  effects of, 28–33
  exposure to, 30–32
  GMOs and, 34
  increased use of, 28, 30, 35
  manufacturers of, 29
  marketing of, 28
  names of, 40
  origins of, 29
  resistance to, 34
Pest management. *See also* Pesticides
  in biodiverse systems, 27, 37–38,
    40, 41
  by industrial agriculture, 27, 28
Pizza Hut, 104
Pollinators
  importance of, xix, 27, 33
  pesticides' effects on, 29, 32, 33
Pollution, xii, 105
Pongam, 38
The Protection of Plant Varieties
  and Farmers' Rights Act, 81
Pusztai, Arpad, 33

Q
Quaker Oats, 59, 104

R
Red Semillas Libres, 81
Research Foundation for Science,
  Technology and Ecology, 35

Return, Law of
  biodiversity and, 47
  food webs and, 61
  living soil and, 20, 24
  localization and, 85–86
  sustainability and, 9–10
  transitioning to, 131–32
Rhône-Poulenc, 29
Rice, golden, 121
Roundup, 32, 34, 35, 36, 73, 121
Royal Society, 114
Rumi, 66
Russia, 39, 61

S
Salatin, Joel, 76
Saptarshi, 53
Sarson (Mustard) Satyagraha, 130
Schieffer, Alexander, 117
Schlosser, Eric, 103
Schmeiser, Percy, 73, 77
Scientific Revolution, 114
Scotland, 75
Seed freedom
  fight for, 79, 82–83
  food democracy and, 138–39
  meaning of, 79–80
  movement for, 81–82
Seeds
  coating of, 30
  companies selling, 70, 86
  corporate control over, 42, 43,
    67–74, 76–79
  cost of, 70
  of farmers' native varieties,
    67–68, 134
  hybrid, 68–69, 120
  importance of, xix, 67, 70, 119
  intellectual property rights and, 75

of knowledge, 137
patents on, 71–74, 76–77, 81
registration of, 75
saving and sharing, 71–72, 75,
    80, 81
terminator, 69
women and, 119–20
Seed Satyagraha, 75, 81
Seed sovereignty, 76, 80, 82, 137
"Seed to table" cycle, 134–38
Sen, Amartya, 119
Separation, Newtonian-Cartesian
    idea of, 4–5, 7
Séralini, Gilles-Éric, 33
Sesbania, 20
Shand, Hope, 73
Sharifa, 38
Shell, 29
Shumei International, 81
Silent Spring (Carson), 28, 29
Singh, Charan, 59–60
Singh, Mohan, 63
Slow Food International, 81
Small-scale farming
    biodiversity and, 56, 61
    crisis for, 63–65
    food security and, 55–56
    importance of, xix, 55–56
    productivity of, 56, 59–63
    transitioning to, 130–31
Soil
    degradation of, 16–17, 25
    fertility of, xix, 17–20, 135
    importance of, xix, 22–24
    as living system, 15–16, 18–20
    microorganisms in, 18–19
    rejuvenating, 134–35
    synthetic fertilizers' effects on, 16

South Africa, ix, 89
Spain, 95
Sugar, 103
Suicides, of farmers, 48, 58–60,
    64–65, 77–79, 107
Summers, Lawrence, 105
Sustainability, 9–11, 49–50
Swadeshi movement, 65
Syngenta, xvii, 37, 86

T
Tagore, Rabindranath, 25
Taittiriya Upanishad, xix
Terminator seeds, 69
Tesco, 86
Thailand, 61
"Three sisters," 53
Tobacco, 38
Trade liberalization, 88–91
TRIPS (Trade-Related Aspects of
    Intellectual Property Rights)
    Agreement, 72–74
Tropicana, 104
Tunisia, ix
Tyson Foods, 86

U
Uganda, 122
Ukraine, 61
UN Convention on Biological
    Diversity, 69
UNCTAD (United Nations
    Conference on Trade and
    Development), 62
Union Carbide, 29, 31
United Kingdom
    food miles in, 106
    hunger in, 96

seed laws in, 75
United Nations Development
  Programme, 120
United States
  agricultural subsidies in, 89
  autism in, 32
  biodiversity loss in, 42
  cancer rates in, 32
  farmers' suicides in, 58–59
  farmland in, 64
  food safety laws in, 76
  GMOs in, 34, 36–37, 39, 72–
    73, 117–18
  hunger in, 96
  loss of fertile soil in, 16
  NAFTA and, 99
  obesity in, 103
  pesticides in, 32, 36
  pollinators in, 33
  seed coating in, 30
UPOV (International Union for the
  Protection of New Varieties on
  Plants), 75
US Department of Agriculture, 38,
  69
US Institute of Medicine, 32

V
Vance, Vicki, 33
Voelcker, John Augustus, 1–2

W
Walmart, 86
Wilkes, H. Garrison, 52
Women
  agricultural systems shaped by,
    xx, 111–12, 114–15, 123–24
  patriarchal economics and, 112–
    13, 116–19
  seed conservation and, 119–20
  violence against, 118–19
  work of, 116–17
Worcester, Tracy, 106
World Bank, xvi, 70, 97, 101, 105,
  119, 120, 135
World Food Programme, 98
World Health Organization
  (WHO), 30, 32, 137
World Trade Organization (WTO),
  72, 78, 86, 88, 92, 97, 109

Z
Zyklon B, 29